IN THE FIELD

IN THE FIELD

Field sports adventures
at home and abroad

ADRIAN DANGAR

Illustrations by Rodger McPhail

Muscoates Publishing

Copyright © 2023 Adrian Dangar

First published in the UK in 2023 by Muscoates Publishing

British Library Cataloguing-in-Publication Data
A catalogue record for this book is available from the British Library

ISBN 978-1-9163100-3-2

The right of Adrian Dangar to be identified as the author of this work has been asserted in accordance with the Copyright, Design and Patent Act 1988.

The Author is indebted to Future Publishing Limited and/or Ti Media for kind permission to reproduce material originally appearing in the pages of *The Field* and *Country Life* magazines.

Front cover photograph by Adrian Dangar.

Illustrations by Rodger McPhail

Design by Becky Bowyer: becky@becbowyer.com

Printed in the UK by Gomer Press

Muscoates Publishing
Muscoates Grange, Nunnington, York YO62 5XF
E-mail: info@muscoatespublishing.com
Website: www.muscoatespublishing.com
Instagram: @adriandangar

Contents

Foreword

THE FIELD WAS a weekly magazine and priced at a princely 60p when Adrian Dangar's byline first appeared in our pages. It was the September 3rd issue 1983, and his report on the Yorkshire Esk held the promise of the writer he would go on to become.

Much has changed over the last 40 years. For starters, as well as picking up *The Field* for a song in 1983, you could also buy 4,000 acres in Scotland that boasted a lodge, deer forest, grouse moor and trout lochs for the price of a modern-day 4x4. Our sporting landscape has undergone similar seismic shifts since then, particularly in the hunting world. However, some things remain pleasingly consistent. Four decades on, Adrian's writing has been a constant for *The Field* and it reads with the same easy elegance and erudition that the author brings to his own sporting life.

What caught the eye of the then Editor is the same that captures my eye today: a genuine enthusiasm for the world within which he lives, a natural curiosity, neat turn of phrase and, of course, the ability to get the job done in a most professional manner – on time, to word count and with accuracy. Adrian is a sincerely valued part of *The Field* family and I have thoroughly appreciated his support since I took over the reins.

This book is a treat to be savoured; part record, part memoir, illustrated with exquisite vignettes by the renowned Rodger McPhail, bringing together the best of our world. There are few writers who have contributed so much to the sporting field. Adrian writes as an enthusiast for enthusiasts, and the contents of this book can be used, by those who wish to, as a handy fieldsports bucket list; one to nod along sagely with or plan to emulate.

Adrian's adventures in the field are all ones on which we'd like to accompany him. This book and its engaging style means that we can.

Alexandra Henton
Editor, *The Field*.

Introduction

THE FIELD PUBLISHED my first article exactly forty years ago, and it has been an absolute privilege to have been allowed to continue writing for Britain's premier field sports magazine ever since. Throughout that time, I have benefitted from the help of numerous features editors, sub-editors and proof-readers and enjoyed the warm camaraderie of a magazine that succeeds in making its writers feel as if they belong to a tight-knit family. I am also grateful to those numerous estate and shoot owners, their tolerant guests, gamekeepers, ghillies, guides, Masters of hounds, hunt staff and field sports professionals the length and breadth of Britain and beyond who have extended such a warm welcome to a *Field* writer on assignment.

I will always be grateful to Derek Bingham, who as Editor back in 1983 was kind enough to accept my first my hand-written effort for publication, but more recently to his successors, Jonathan Young and Alexandra Henton. During JY's long innings at the helm he was kind enough to wing some exhilarating – and challenging – commissions my way, which were invariably accompanied by the stern reminder that failure was not an option. It was thanks to him that I was able to achieve a Macnab (regrettably not poached), shoot an English wild boar and flight pinkfeet geese beneath a full moon onto the hallowed coursing grounds at Altcar. Alexandra Henton, who took over the reins in 2020, has been equally generous and accommodating, sending me as far away as Chilean Patagonia on assignment and, like her predecessor, perennially receptive to my field sports ideas and feature proposals.

These, and other hand-picked "Fieldy" adventures spanning four decades, are reproduced here, along with three that came my way courtesy of *The Field's* sister publication, *Country Life*, with which I have also enjoyed a long and happy relationship. Each chapter represents a full-length feature as originally captioned for publication, and is preceded by a few lines of personal and retrospective observations in italics.

The icing on the cake of this book is provided by the vignettes painted specially for each chapter by the supremely talented wildlife artist, Rodger McPhail. I have admired Rodger's work from afar for as long as I can remember, and could not believe my good fortune when he kindly agreed to illustrate *In The Field*. Not only did he execute each sketch with an uncanny ability to encapsulate the accompanying text, he also produced them months ahead of schedule.

This is the third of my books designed by Becky Bowyer, who is a pleasure to work with, skilled at her job and a constant source of guidance and advice. Becky also designed the front cover, which features my two terriers overlooking a Yorkshire landscape that is home to many of the emblematic species that feature in the book. I chose this image not just for the all-encompassing English landscape it portrays, but also because – at least anywhere in the UK – the terriers are my constant companions in the hunting field, out shooting and on the riverbank. This is the second of my books that the eagle-eyed Hampshire sportsman, John Cavendish, has most kindly proofread, and I hope it will not be the last.

It remains only for me to thank you, the reader, for taking the time to peruse this book, and more importantly to continuing reading *The Field* each month, where you will be kept abreast of all that is going on the world of field sports and our cherished rural way of life.

Adrian Dangar
August 2023

PART ONE

HORSE & HOUND

Hounds move off at last

A morning with the VWH in Cirencester Park,
December 2001

*I remember this assignment as it if were yesterday. No one had been hunting
since the countryside had been closed by an outbreak of foot and mouth
the previous winter, and few believed the suspension would be lifted before
Christmas 2001. The VWH were one of the first hunts to get off the mark
after the green light had been given to resume hunting. The Field's features
Editor, Lucy Higginson, telephoned me the previous day and asked if I could
go out with the Gloucestershire-based hunt and file copy within 24 hours. In
retrospect the joyous December morning that followed proved to be something
of a false dawn, for within four years the invidious Hunting Act would become
law and hunting would never be the same again. Sidney Bailey retired at
the end of the 2004–2005 season having carried the VWH horn for over
40 years and served 23 different Masters. I was privileged to be amongst the*

300 mounted followers at Cirencester Park who came to pay tribute to Sidney on his last day carrying the horn. The sight of the VWH hounds and their huntsman riding his favourite grey horse to the meet down a colourful guard of honour formed by past and present hunt staff and Masters is one I will never forget.

IF THE PROFESSIONAL huntsman to the Vale of White Horse Hunt in Gloucestershire felt any pressure on the morning of December 17th 2001, his first day back in action since the suspension of hunting due to an outbreak of foot and mouth disease the previous February, he concealed it well. During thirty-six years of service to this hunt Sidney Bailey had never begun a hunting season in mid-winter before, nor attended an opening meet at 9am surrounded by riders in ratcatcher, a concession in dress to reflect the unique circumstances of the occasion. Everyone present at Lord Bathurst's estate on that frosty December morning was participating in an historic event, a resumption of hunting that the pessimists had forecast would not take place at all this season, and one that even a month earlier had looked unlikely.

In choosing to stage their comeback within the extensive woodlands of Cirencester Park the Masters of the VWH had not only selected a near-perfect environment in which a rusty pack could spend its first morning, but also an ethereal setting to match the significance of the event; as horses gathered, enveloped by clouds of vapour, a fine wintry sun threw long shadows across the famous polo field, and singed the tips of the tall cedars beyond a fiery yellow. Looking back towards Cirencester down one of the many wide avenues that dissect the old woodlands the silhouette of the town's 12th century church stood out cleanly against a leaden sky.

It was against this backdrop that the longest-serving of the four VWH Joint Masters, Mark Hill, rose in his stirrups to address the crowd. Whilst delighted to welcome the overdue start of a new season, he urged co-operation with the foot and mouth restrictions in force, and thanked Francesca Drummond, the disease centre manager at Gloucester, for her efforts in ensuring that the local hunts were able to collect their licences in time to begin hunting as soon as restrictions were lifted.

Moments later Sidney was trotting off to the first draw, surrounded by his exuberant pack, and followed by an equally enthusiastic field. As we jogged across the park Mark explained the complicated procedures which had to be unravelled before hunting could begin. Firstly the hunt had to supply maps, lists, names and addresses to the DEFRA office in Gloucester. Lengthy meetings and discussions followed, culminating with the issuing of essential licences five days in advance of December 17th. Contrary to what may have been expected from a department whose government is openly hostile to field sports, the Gloucestershire hunts found DEFRA happy to assist. "Mrs Drummond and her team have been incredibly helpful and co-operative," Mark revealed, "once we had received a licence to hunt we then had to issue certificates of compliance to every subscriber and member for signatures; we posted these, together with information, guidelines and a meet card, to over 800 addresses."

That the VWH was able to start hunting so promptly was thanks to both accommodating government officials and a dedicated team of Masters. There can be few better qualified for the position than Mark Hill, who began his hunting career with the VWH as whipper-in to Sidney Bailey in 1980 under the mastership of Martin Scott. "He was always in the right place, very polite, and I cannot remember him putting a foot wrong," is how Martin, who continues to breed the VWH pack to this day, remembers him. After Cirencester and marriage into a local hunting and farming dynasty Mark returned to take on the role of Secretary in 1988, and joined the mastership in 1997. He is assisted by Charles Mann, who together with his wife Chips has worked tirelessly for the Campaign for Hunting, and Christine Mason, a farmer's wife who runs the Monday side and provides her field with a fearless lead across country. The newest member of the team, lifelong VWH supporter and farmer, Martin Wood, was enjoying his first day's hunting as an MFH.

The Hunt is especially fortunate to have the extensive woodlands of Cirencester Park within the western portion of its country, and to enjoy strong support from the Bathurst family; Alexander Bathurst was amongst the large, mounted field, and his sister in law Lady Apsley's robust stance in challenging the government over their handling of the foot and mouth crisis has won her many admirers in the countryside. As was soon evidenced by the grin on Bailey's face, these woods are a huntsman's delight; well foxed and accessible they provide a place of refuge in times of hard weather and extend the season by several weeks in spring. "The big woods have not always been popular with previous Masters," explained Christine Mason, who as Monday Master was in charge of the day, "but I love them, and the harder we hunt them, the better the foxes travel. A month or two into every season we have some really good hunts from the park."

The VWH country has been hunted since the beginning of the 19th century, however the title of Vale of White Horse was not assumed until 1831. In 1886 a fierce row divided the country that led to the formation of two separate packs under the respective masterships of Earl Bathurst and Charles Hoare (Cricklade). The two countries were not reunited until 1964, and peace has reigned ever since. The present country affords sufficient space to hunt a varied landscape four days a week. In the north, where the boundary marches with the Heythrop, light brash soil characterises the higher ground. This is an area of wide spaces, stout foxes and big shooting estates, nearly all of which accommodate the Hunt. To the south, and bordering the Duke of Beaufort's and Old Berkshire, lie the remnants of a challenging heavy grass vale, much of which is now under the plough. However enduring pockets of old-fashioned turf still provide the VWH field with tremendous fun when hounds run the right way.

With such illustrious neighbours the VWH has always been in the best of company, but the hunt also enjoys loyal support, much of it from the farming community. It was typical of the VWH's spirit that many supporters had spent the previous day tramping the streets of Edinburgh to protest Watson's anti-hunting bill. Despite the gravity of the situation, the mood amongst the VWH contingent in Scotland had been buoyant; Guy Dibble, a farmer from the Thursday country, spoke for many when he told me, "I can hardly wait to start hunting again tomorrow." Julian Weston who runs an agricultural machinery business went further, "our hounds are out every day next week, and so am I," he boasted, "the business can wait, it's only stock taking in the run-up to Christmas." In choosing to hunt six days out of the first seven available, the Joint Masters have signalled their determination to make up for lost time. By meeting at 9am and finishing by early afternoon hunt staff will have sufficient time to perform essential duties against a backdrop of two days' extra hunting each week.

When the huntsman reached Wellhill, a long straggling covert of thick brambles beneath a canopy of tall beeches, he paused to give the field time to line the far side and prevent hounds from running into open country on their first day for ten months. In the silence that followed it seemed that everyone was holding their breath. Minutes trickled by slowly, with only the metallic twang of the horn and the huntsman's familiar cheer betraying the presence of 22½ couple, and then the magical moment we had been waiting for since last February: the staccato note of a bitch owning the line of a fox. One voice was quickly two, and within a minute the music of hounds in full cry reverberated across the wintry landscape. No one could have captured the mood better than Sidney Bailey as he trotted past in the wake of his pack roaring on the line of their first fox of the season. Moving his head slowly in wonder, his cheery face wreathed in smiles, he exclaimed softly beneath his breath, "marvellous, bloody marvellous."

The pack chiming away through the woodlands was chiefly made up of experienced doghounds but included a smattering of bitches and just two couple of puppies. Knowing that second season hounds have the potential to cause the most trouble, Sidney had left many of that generation behind for this first day's hunting in nearly a year. His judgement was vindicated as the pack rattled up and down the belt with at least two brace in front, as onlookers contemplated the irony of a lost autumn hunting campaign against the sight of a laid-off pack hunting like seasoned professionals. Shortly after ten o'clock the VWH hounds caught their first fox of the season and went on to add a leash to the tally during a morning when their quarry exploded from every covert. After four glorious hours of unbroken hunting with a pack that cannot have been more than half fit, their huntsman was persuaded to blow reluctantly for home.

"That dark 'un's wheezed 'im..."

A day with the Farndale, January 2003

*When hunting the Sinnington hounds in the 1990s I was frequently impressed by the remarkable hunts achieved by the Farndale, whose rough moorland country lay to the north of our own manicured territory. Its followers were hound men and women to the core and included many of the local grouse moor gamekeepers. A hunt whose sole purpose was to provide fox control was never going to flourish after the Hunting Act became law, but this tiny pack limped on for another decade. By then many of the keepers mentioned in the text below had moved on and been replaced by men from afar who knew little of the Farndale Hunt's traditions and importance to the local community. The Farndale's final meet on March 14*th *2014 was without doubt the saddest sporting occasion I have ever attended. The largest mounted field for years and over 200 foot followers turned up to pay their final respects to a hunt that had endured in one form or another ever since the Duke of Buckingham's hounds first hunted the surrounding moorland*

in 1790. To add insult to injury, saboteurs had got wind of the event and their presence persuaded the Farndale shooting tenant to forbid hounds from moving off. A more ignominious finale for a once flourishing hunt would be hard to conceive.

FLICKING THROUGH THE pages of a 1935 edition of *Baily's Hunting Directory* I can find only one hunt listed as trencher fed – the term refers to hounds that are not kennelled together, but rather looked after individually by supporters and brought together to form a pack on hunting days. Instead of a kennels address for the Farndale Hunt in North Yorkshire, the text reveals nothing save the blunt description: "8 couple of trencher fed hounds." I have not trawled hunting's annual encyclopaedia for details of every hunt registered, however by the late nineteenth century the nearby Bilsdale, Cleveland and Sinnington Hunts had all converted from the trencher fed system. The foot packs of fell hounds in the Lake District made the change even earlier – the famous Blencathra in 1826, the Coniston in 1853 and the Melbreak in 1807.

No one connected with the present Farndale can tell me exactly when their fell-bred hounds came to be kennelled under one roof, however lifelong supporter and Ravenswick gamekeeper Stephen Todd remembers his uncle George loosing his hound off on hunting mornings in the Forties, "Jack Shaw used to blow for the pack in Farndale and everyone for miles around just let their hounds out to go and find him – at night they used to wander off home again. In them days folk used to go trailing with their hounds in summer, and foxhunting in winter."

Currently kennelled at their huntsman Brian Marshall's smallholding near Stape, the Farndale still send over half the pack back to where they were walked as puppies for the long summer months. "Anyone walking a puppy knows that hound is theirs for life," says Brian of such characters as Frank Croft, Colin Newlove, Jane Short, Stephen Todd, Andrew Lander and the Tinsley family – all gamekeepers or farmers, united by their love for hunting and fell hounds. The only hound qualifying as a true trencher fed member of the pack this season is Hamlet, a tricolour doghound that resides with Joint Master George Atkinson on his hill farm at Kildale. "He fell down Spaunton quarry and hurt his foot, so he stops back home with me now, and I bring him out once a week," George explains.

The Feversham Arms is an appropriate venue for me to join the Farndale for a mid-week hunt, and not just because this small pub lies at the very heart of the dale from which the Hunt takes its name. The Feversham family, whose name is also synonymous with the neighbouring Sinnington Hunt, once owned a huge slice of the Farndale's country. "My family have always supported the Farndale, and I am honoured to have followed my mother as chairman – hopefully my son Freddie, who has recently come back here to live, will also become involved," Lady Clarissa Colin told me. Her mother, the Countess of Feversham, compiled the magical book *Strange Stories of the Chase* whilst Joint Master of the Sinnington.

When I arrive at the pub ten minutes ahead of the appointed hour I find the bar inside packed with men dressed in tweeds and stout leather boots. A quick exercise in mental arithmetic puts the land under the collective management of these gamekeepers at close to fifty thousand acres, and I wonder how many other hunts could possibly draw such support from their local shoots. When an upturned cap does the rounds, big hands ferret out coins from deep pockets to contribute to the finances of a hunt that costs just £6,000 a year to run. Back in 1935 no capping at all was practised but a mounted visitor is now asked to contribute £15 to ride behind the Farndale pack, and £40 for a full season's sport.

When hounds move off they are accompanied by just four riders, including Joint Master Hilary Mintoft and Jane Short, whose husband Colin is headkeeper to the Bransdale estate. Many prefer to follow the Farndale on foot or by car, and for the next twenty minutes we stand outside the pub, grateful for a chance to digest the landlady's thick slabs of beef pie whilst we watch hounds at work on the dark hillside towering above us. Mist is clinging like a grey shroud to the highest ground, and as the pack spread out to draw across rafts of sodden bracken and dirty brown heather, a line of black-faced sheep scurry off into the gloom. Down in the valley floor a thrush sings brightly from the branches of an alder tree. "Spring is on the way," proclaims one follower optimistically.

Hounds disappearing are the cue for Joint Master George Atkinson and myself to trudge uphill through fields of saturated pasture to the Bracken Banks. Bilty Kearsley, a retired lorry driver who has followed the Farndale for forty years, joins us for the walk. Bilty travels thirty miles to hunt here. "When my local hunt meet outside our house on Boxing Day I never even look at them – I come straight to the Farndale. I like hunting in open country," he tells me. The Bracken Banks sprawl along the side of Farndale and are pockmarked with rocky outcrops and heaps of broken granite scattered haphazardly about the hillside. If ever there was a place for hill foxes to live, it is here, sheltered from the prevailing westerlies by Blakey Ridge, and rarely disturbed by the local shoot or its headkeeper, Frank Croft. The Farndale have a true friend in Frank, who not only takes hounds home for the summer, but also does everything he can to ensure the hunt have a good day when they visit his patch. "All field sports have to stick together, and we do take great pride in providing sport for the hunt when they are here, and they in turn provide a good service by catching foxes for us," he tells me.

The view from the Bracken Banks across Farndale is nothing short of breathtaking – the stonework of the closest walls glinting like fish scales in the watery light, and those farther away running in thin grey lines across tired pastures to meet the heather on distant Horn Ridge. My eye is drawn to the sound of plashing water, and a frayed white ribbon seething angrily down the face of a granite precipice. Below us a farmer is calling out noisily to his flock of sheep, quite oblivious to the presence of a pack of hounds at work on the fellside above him. Life does not stop here for the Farndale hounds, which are as deeply rooted in the landscape as the wild red grouse chortling from the heather. As the rain begins to patter down, terrierman Bryan Kidd hurries past, towed along by two white terriers secured together at the neck by chain couplings.

A couple of hounds appear from around the shoulder of the hillside, sterns lashing busily. "That dark 'un's wheezed 'im", observes George Atkinson, who has been a hill farmer all his life, and a Master of the Farndale for the past eleven seasons. Moments later we hear Wisdom's deep booming voice, and hounds come cascading out of the heather to take up the scent, and quickly vanish from sight. Within ten minutes we catch the sound of their voices on the breeze, and George spots a lithe brown shape slipping over the granite wall below us. When hounds mark to ground amongst boulders the size of a tractor, the huntsman appears on his feet and signals for a terrier to be released. The dog disappears underground baying furiously, and excited holloaing signals the fox's departure.

Hounds marking for a second time give me an opportunity to talk hunting and hounds with the huntsman, referred to by everyone as Shoaly, an affectionate reference to his propensity for parting company with his mount when amateur whipper-in to the adjacent Saltersgate Hunt. These dales retain a dialect and vocabulary of their own and the verb shoal – as in fall – is just one example of a unique and colourful language holding out against extinction in the 21st century. Shoaly, who works as a joiner and carpenter, is no great fan of the horse. "I'd rather be hunting these hounds on me feet really – the country's that rough and boggy that you can't draw where you want to. Half the time you 'ave to ride out around bogs and that – someone takes me horse and I walks through." Shoaly has his horse and hounds to attend to when he gets home at night, and he never misses the opportunity to save the hunt money. "I don't buy shoes for me horse," he says, "I prize them off dead ones at the knacker's yard." Hounds are fed cheaply, but well, on a diet of raw flesh, bakery waste and cracked eggs from a nearby poultry farm. "We get seventy dozen a week, we put 'em in a bucket, smash 'em up and pour 'em over the bakery waste, the hounds love it – they gobble down shells 'an all," he says.

The best hunt of the day begins when a handful of old hounds wander off as we wait for the hunted fox to bolt, and evict a fox on their own from another jumble of rocks several hundred yards away. We are treated to tantalising glimpses of the pack's progress as they stream in and out of sight through the folds of the surrounding hills, and 50 minutes later we hear them marking to ground above the grey cloud line on the west side of Blakey Gill. What follows is the low point in an otherwise outstanding day, but to retrieve any pack of hounds by holloaing them back to hunt an imaginary fox is the worst form of deception, and a practice that no pack will stomach for long. The performance disturbs me, but the men of these dales have their own way of doing things, and I watch in silence as hounds come loping back from the earth.

Hounds are hurriedly loaded into the rear of assorted vehicles, and driven three miles back to the Bracken Banks. Although Master and huntsman are keen to account for this fox, clearly nothing is going to evict him – experts are sure that it is the dog fox hounds hunted so beautifully out to Blakey Gill – and as the crepuscular glow of dusk draws a veil down over the valley, we leave that fox to run another day, and begin our long, slippery descent off the hillside.

Legacy of a legend lives on

Autumn hunting with the Exmoor, September 2003

This article is one of three I have included that were commissioned by Country Life *magazine. It is a remarkable tribute to the Exmoor's continuity that Felicita Busby MFH and her huntsman, Tony Wright, are both still in office twenty years on. The Exmoor landscape has altered little in the intervening years, however there has been an increase in shooting for hunts to contend with, not to mention the Hunting Act, which became law less than eighteen months after the morning described. The Stars of the West are no longer as prominent on the flags as they were during Captain Wallace's long reign at the helm, but they continue to provide fine sport across timeless moorland vistas that still attract hunting visitors from all over Britain and beyond.*

IT IS JUST a few minutes after 6am, and I am sitting on my horse looking out across the Barle Valley towards Withypool. The river flowing hundreds of feet below me is concealed beneath a lake of dense mist, which is slowly draining from the surrounding coombes to reveal hillsides smothered in thick bracken. As the rising sun burnishes the underbellies of clouds to the east in a golden glow, the first shafts of light fall on the purple summit of Withypool Common away to the south. The view is glorious, but even better is the tinkle of music made by the Exmoor hounds unravelling the overnight drag of a moorland fox.

The scene and landscape are familiar to lovers of hunting from all over the world. Names such as Pickedstones, Honeymead and Hawkridge not only recall memories of great hunts from the past, but they are also synonymous with the Exmoor's late and legendary Master, Captain Ronnie Wallace, who hunted and bred this famous pack of hounds – also called the Stars of the West – for 25 seasons. His death two years ago sent shock waves through the hunting community and left the Exmoor Hunt devoid of their influential leader; but no one familiar with his flair for organisation should be the least surprised to learn that he had prepared his hunt for this eventuality many years earlier. "When I gave up the West Somerset, the Captain suggested I come and hunt with him," explains Felicita Busby, who is starting her eleventh season as the Exmoor's Joint Master. "I had no idea he was weighing me up that first season, but the following year he invited me to join the mastership. He told me I was good with people, and crossed the country well – although too fast."

Miss Busby now describes herself as "one hundred percent more enthusiastic" than when she first started, and spends her days either out hunting, or assisting at the kennels and stables in a hands-on role. Despite her nine years' experience alongside Captain Wallace, taking on the mantle of Senior Master was a daunting prospect. "Of course, I had been well prepared," she explains, "but I had no idea if I was going to be capable of doing the job without him. He always impressed on me the importance of maintaining the hunt's standards – he worried they would slip after he had gone. The Captain's greatest legacies have been our huntsman, Tony Wright, and the hounds themselves. It's a tremendous privilege to be involved."

During the morning I was able to observe those legacies at close quarters, and I was not disappointed. The drag hounds hit off within minutes of leaving the meet led us upstream into Pickedstones – a steep plantation of tall pines flanked by wild tangles of briar and bracken. Here, several foxes kept the pack occupied for over ninety minutes, including several excursions into the open. Tony Wright enjoys an extraordinary rapport with his hounds, and was on hand to offer help whenever needed. Economical with voice, horn and horse, his quiet, unhurried manner is devastatingly effective. Whether it be nudging the pack quarter of a mile onto clean ground, cheering them softly as they recover the line, or trotting back to retrieve hounds with nothing more than a low whistle, he exudes an aura of unshakeable confidence. This is a man with whom every aspiring huntsman should have a day.

After the pack's perseverance was rewarded, we crossed the Barle to draw the brackeny slopes on the south bank, choosing a place only a few hundred yards downstream from where the Devon and Somerset had taken their stag after a fine hunt the previous evening. The stag and foxhound packs on Exmoor are used to welcoming visitors to a landscape that the artist Cecil Aldin described as the riding playground of England. The most popular times are late summer, before hunting in other parts of Britain has begun, and again in springtime after sport up country has finished for the season. On this morning visitors included John Chatfeild-Roberts, his wife Doone, and their two young sons learning about hunting away from the hurly-burly of days in high Leicestershire where they live.

Regular followers included Biddy Trouton and Penny Crane. The latter was also accompanied by her son Patrick, and Mrs Trouton – complete with a red collar identifying her as Loveday Miller's assistant Secretary – spent all morning leaping energetically on and off her smart grey to open gates. The field also included Liz Verity, formerly Master of the Bramham Moor in Yorkshire, and another of Captain Wallace's shrewd recruits to the Exmoor mastership. Mrs Verity first hunted on Exmoor with her father as a teenager, and now has responsibility for liaising with farmers over the hunt's movements – not an easy task in this wild country. "Holding foxes up here is impossible, and we are just as likely to have a four-mile point in mid-August as mid season," she says, "but our farmers are fantastic, and very understanding."

When a crash of music signals a fox well found above the Barle, expectations for a hunt are high, and Miss Busby is quick to gallop after the pack climbing out over Great Woolcombe. "I don't like to be on the opposite side of a valley to hounds, because if they go out over the top that could be the last I see of them and Tony for the rest of the day," she laughs.

By now the dew has evaporated and although hounds stick determinedly to their fox, it is clear we are not going to get a long hunt – although another fox is added to the tally before the morning draws to a natural close. As we hack home through hazy heat, we pass Lady Caroline Gosling following on foot. A former Exmoor Joint Master, she is now responsible for breeding this distinguished pack, yet another detail the Captain did not neglect.

After a classic morning's autumn hunting – my first with the Exmoor since Captain Wallace's death – I have a visit to make before going home to breakfast. The churchyard at Simonsbath is deserted, but I have no difficulty in finding the famous foxhunter's grave, inscribed with the names of the nine packs of hounds he hunted continuously from 1939 until shortly before his death. The headstone stands in the north-eastern corner of the churchyard – the very place foxes like to cross when hunted by the Exmoor hounds.

Middleton hunting goes high-octane

A day with Middleton, November 2003

The Middleton enjoyed something of a golden era during the mastership of Frank Houghton-Brown and this was a typical day in the cream of their country. Having completed fourteen successful seasons at the helm of Yorkshire's only remaining four-days-a-week pack, Frank moved to the Tynedale Hunt in Northumberland in 2004. Otis Ferry went on to make a name for himself, firstly as one of the Westminster Eight who broke into the House of Commons in September 2004 to protest the Hunting Act, and later as Master and huntsman to the South Shropshire. Twenty years on, the Middleton Hunt continue to show fine sport across their beautiful and expansive North Yorkshire countryside.

THE MIDDLETON FIELD are jostling in a muddy ride, and chattering like magpies after the first burst of the day, their horses lathered in sweat and raring to be on with the hunt. Ten minutes earlier the bitch pack had found a fox in Wheathills — a lovely thick covert with rafts of old man's beard draped across withering brambles, straggles of laid hawthorn and larch trees dripping golden needles onto the woodland floor. Now there is confusion as some hounds have killed a fox in Thackers, leaving half the pack running hard on another. As the huntsman rounds the corner you can see him straining to decipher their cry above the noisy murmur of elated riders. He pulls his horse up short, stands up in the stirrups, and colours the air blue with invective. The background chatter shuts out like a light, and suddenly we can hear hounds hunting once more, and a spine-tingling holloa signalling a fox away from the furthest corner of the wood.

This is high-octane hunting with the Middleton in the cream of their country, hunt staff as finely tuned to their roles as the hounds themselves, a Master who has been up since dawn taking down the last strands of wire, and expectations running high after recent rains have softened the going for the first time this season. Clearly, we are not out for a stroll in the proverbial. Seconds later the pack are streaming away from Thackers, and we meet the first of many hedges — a black barricade that the field attack with gusto. A handful fail to make it, and their loose horses career wildly into the distance. Meanwhile hounds have crossed the Leppington lane onto bare arable, where a lone bitch hangs on tenaciously to the line as her colleagues swoop wide in a fruitless cast. Hearing her voice, they race uphill to join her with a crash of music that surely quickens the pace of their quarry slipping through boggy pastures a quarter of a mile in front. Twenty minutes later the pack mark their fox to ground to conclude the second hunt of the day.

Since his appointment as Joint Master and huntsman to the Middleton fourteen seasons ago, Frank Houghton-Brown has fashioned his hunt into one that enjoys an enviable reputation for superb sport and high standards. Throughout that time he has hunted hounds four days a week across the biggest hunting country in Yorkshire, one that stretches inland from the North Sea, across bleak chalk wolds to the fertile Farlington Vale in the west, a distance of over forty miles. This is a landscape of grand estates — Sledmere, Garrowby, Birdsall and Castle Howard all fall within the hunt's boundary — and some serious shooting. "We are fortunate to enjoy such support from Garrowby and Birdsall, two estates that march side by side and run to over 30,000 acres between them, but elsewhere it's not so easy.

During my time here dozens of new shoots have started up, and the pressure of arranging hunting to fit in with all of them has intensified," Frank explains as we trot on to draw Leppington Wood.

Although we do touch Lord Halifax's Garrowby acres, much of the day is to be spent on George Winn-Darley's land surrounding Aldby Park. A supporter of all field sports, George had appeared briefly at the Paces' hospitable meet in Scrayingham to deliver a shooting guest's wife for her day's hunting aboard one of Judy Thurloe's hirelings. The close proximity of a shooting party is a familiar scenario for the Middleton in recent years; perhaps less usual is our host's relaxed attitude – "if we meet up with his shoot, George won't mind in the slightest," says Frank with a wry smile – "we're incredibly lucky to have landowners as helpful as him." Houghton-Brown is also fortunate to have farmers Mary Rook, Richard Mason and William Bradley as his Joint Masters, whose contribution to the complex organisation of hunting in a heavily shot country is described as "invaluable."

The excitement is palpable as dairy farmer Stuart Wood opens his farmyard gate to welcome us onto his acres of rolling grassland, and as we ride through Peter McColgan, the Middleton's popular kennel huntsman, pauses to give him a brief report on the puppy he has walked for the hunt. Elsewhere Jeff Wood senior is following by bicycle – his preferred form of conveyance on hunting days. Just when it seems that the covert will be drawn blank, we are off again to the accompaniment of splintering timber, pounding hooves, and the chiming music of the Middleton bitches. The pace slackens as we hit a broad belt of arable on the edge of Garrowby, and the field receive their second admonishment of the day – this time from Simon Roberts. When he demands, "can I have your attention please?" the Field Master commands instant respect from mud-splattered riders that for the last thirty minutes have ridden hard in his wake.

"My style of field mastering is to keep as close as I can to the action," he says quietly, "but to do that I require absolute silence when we are near to the hounds." As a former Master and huntsman of the neighbouring Derwent, Roberts understands exactly when to make his move – and equally important, when to hold back and give hounds space to work. "During most hunts there is a narrow window of opportunity when you can show the field real fun, and then you just have to go for it," he says. It is true nothing disrupts a hound's concentration more than noise – which is why every huntsman dreads mobs of screaming antis – and in this corner of North Yorkshire the doctrine of silence is adhered to with almost religious fervour. Nothing is allowed to interfere with the pack's concentration – even the practice of shouting, "gate please" is discouraged. Instead the field communicate with each other by a series of hand signals that everyone appears to understand.

The fox finds refuge close to the Barthorpe road, where the view towards Garrowby is a vista of old-fashioned England – a broad spread of wintry pastures dotted with hedgerow oaks rising towards famous coverts hanging from distant hillsides. At their foot we can make out a black smudge that is Garrowby Preserves, perhaps the most celebrated Middleton covert of them all. As we pause to change horses, Eric Wheatman drives up and passes round a bottle of port – the farmer is a lifelong supporter of the hunt, and helps organise country west of the busy A64, including the once delectable Farlington Vale. Eric's passenger is Anne Henson, a former Master who in 1990 traced a missing bloodline to the Galway Blazer kennels in Ireland. That line is one of four stemming from Warwickshire Comfort 1820, a bitch from which over half the present pack are descended. Kennelled on the Birdsall estate since 1853, these hounds were once criticised for their heavy shoulders, but the use of stallion hounds from Badminton, together with an infusion of hill blood from the College Valley in Northumberland, has produced a pack that not only hunt well, but also perform with distinction on the flags.

Hacking on to the next draw provides an opportunity to chat to those who are wise enough to have organised a second horse, amongst them brewer Charles Dent and his daughter, Sarah, blissfully unaware that she is destined to end the day unconscious in a farmer's kitchen after taking a crashing fall over the Leppington hedges. Others include farmer Colin Milburn, who whips-in as an amateur twice a week, and Otis Ferry, son of the famous singer, Brian. Otis relishes his job as the hunt's second whipper-in, and is determined to make hunting his life. "With such incredible pro-hunting drive from our farmers, landowners and supporters, I've never felt insecure about the future of hunting up here," he says.

"I'll just run 'em through this – you never know," says Houghton-Brown cheering hounds into a patch of mustard sown as a covert crop for shooting, which to everyone's delight holds a fox. The afternoon air is cooler now, and hounds leave the mustard going like scalded cats for Lawson Thorns, where pickers-up from George Winn-Darley's shoot had been busy a few hours earlier. Riders wait like coiled springs as hound rattle round the thorn covert, and then we are galloping in the wake of the flying pack, and suddenly squaring up to a long line of inviting fences. The fourth hedge claims the huntsman as one of several victims, and when my own horse finds a fifth leg to avoid trampling his prostrate body, blacksmith Robert Tierney jokes as he gallops past, "I know you want his job, but there's no need to kill him."

It takes more than a fall to keep Houghton-Brown down, and before hounds cross the Scrayingham to Barthorpe road he is again riding in hard pursuit. Our fox runs three miles straight back to Leppington, crossing Stuart Wood's lovely grass farm for a second time, and giving an already sated field the most challenging ride of the day. A check behind the village provides respite for tired horses, not to mention their riders. Richard Charles is grinning from ear to ear as he approaches, "You don't expect as good a day as this in November – is this better than sex?" he drools. Other survivors include Nick Lane Fox, John Cottingham, Stuart Easby, and Tristan Voorspuy, who is more at home galloping across the plains of Africa than riding to hounds in Yorkshire.

Just when defeat seems unavoidable there is a distant holloa, and the huntsman hurries to the sound – when we get there, I realise that only the hunt staff and Field Master are left from a field of over seventy riders, but hounds struggle with a cold line, and home is blown in the gathering dusk. Half an hour later I pass Tim Lambeth, a huntsman visiting from New Zealand, waiting in the dark for his lift. I wind down my window to ask what he thought of the day. He looks a little bemused, even shell shocked. "You guys do it differently to us," he says and grins.

Duffing up foxes in Wales
A day with the Cŵn Paxton, November 2003

I enjoyed my outing with this Welsh gun pack only two weeks after my high-octane day with the Middleton, and the contrast could not have been greater. At the time hopes were still high that a sustainable future for hunting could be secured in Westminster, although no one was pressing for guns to be part of the equation in lowland Britain. After this article was published a reader wrote to Simon Hart, who was then chief executive of the Countryside Alliance, expressing his fervent hope that gun packs would never be considered part of the solution. I expect the high profile field sports campaigners copied into his correspondence would have agreed at the time, however I suspect their reaction would be different twenty years later. Former Welsh Secretary and current Chief Whip, Simon Hart MP, and I shared a cottage when we were students at Cirencester, where he hunted the RAC Beagles. Simon went on to hunt the South Pembrokeshire; during those years it would have been hard to find anyone more dedicated to the chase.

I HAD NO idea where the Editor's invitation to follow up "a bobbery pack, privately maintained to duff up the local fox population," would lead, but I should have guessed it would be Wales. Research there did not uncover a scruffy bobbery pack, but instead the impeccably organised Cŵn Paxton, formed in 1990 to hunt sixty square miles of Carmarthenshire countryside, and fill the void left by the disbanded Spitre Farmers. Fortunately, local sheep and dairy farmer Keith Jones had been given a few of their best hounds to help out his neighbours with fox control, so not only was the nucleus of the new pack already in place, but there was also someone willing and able to take on the role of Master and huntsman.

However, there is a fundamental difference between the Paxton and any other hunt I have ever been out with. Their subscribers follow on foot – nothing particularly unusual about that – but they also carry shotguns to shoot any fox that comes within range. Setting aside my own old-fashioned belief that the proper way to kill a fox is with a pack of hounds, I remembered only too well stories of strife and feuding in the Welsh hills, as mounted hunts and gun packs clashed in disputes over country. Conventional hunts viewed gun packs as little more than bloodthirsty pirates, whereas the gunmen accused their detractors of gross inefficiency, and reminded them just how many foxes they killed each year.

Before heading west, I asked Simon Hart for an update on fox hunting in the Principality, and he explained some of the many changes that have taken place since those days of open warfare; as a former Master of the South Pembrokeshire and a resident of Carmarthenshire, there are few better qualified to comment than the Countryside Alliance's chief executive. "There were so many gun packs operating in Wales that pretending they didn't exist was ridiculous," he told me. "Their followers are natural supporters of hunting, not enemies, and we agreed there are many different way to control foxes, which are regarded as vermin here. In 1989 a group of us representing different hunting interests in Wales formed the Federation of Welsh Packs to reduce the constant competition between hunts and help create unity."

Eight years ago, gun packs joined the Independent Supervisory Authority on Hunting, the body set up to regulate hunting with hounds in Britain, and the Federation drew up a code of conduct, which has improved relationships between hunts in Wales. According to Simon Hart, "thanks in no small part to the Federation and the involvement of ISAH, packs such as the Paxton co-operate with mounted hunts, which in turn recognise the role fulfilled by gun packs."

No one exemplifies this spirit of co-operation better than Keith Jones, who although recovering from an injury, followed his hunt's progress by vehicle throughout the day. The farmer and former point-to-point trainer looks after twenty-five couple of Welsh and Welsh x English hounds on his farm, within sight of the tall stone monument after which the hunt is named. "We have a good relationship with our neighbours," he confirmed, "last year I enjoyed two days mounted with the Carmarthenshire, and in the past have even been asked to hunt country ahead of them before they meet." Foxes abound in this corner of Carmarthenshire, where lamping in dense forestry is impossible, and government rangers no longer set snares. There is more hunting here than anywhere else in Britain, and yet the Paxton regularly account for over 300 foxes a year, and in the 1999–2000 season killed 360.

My day with the Paxton starts inside the Forest Arms in Brechfa, where I find hunt supporters gathered round a blazing fire watching England beat Australia in the World Cup final. Perhaps not the most opportune moment to effect introductions, but I am welcomed warmly, and a glass of scotch is pressed into my hand. Half an hour later men lugging shotguns and wearing faded waterproofs, woollen hats, and thick socks peeled down over gumboot tops are striding up a hillside as hounds wait inside the van, their sterns lashing eagerly against the aluminium sides. When Aled Davies receives word that everyone is in position, the chairman and deputy huntsman drops the tailgate and cheers hounds into thick brambles at Llystyn. I follow the hunt terrierman, Eirian George, who is accompanied by his wirehaired terriers and a lean lurcher bitch. "We pay just £20 a year to be a member of the hunt, which is not bad for a season's sport. We meet every Saturday and Sunday, plus the first Tuesday of each month – so far I've not missed a day this season," he says.

The first wood is surprisingly blank, and we follow a deep brown valley steaming with mist on our way to 14,500 acres of mostly pine trees that comprise Brechfa forestry. As the view unfolds the difficulty of controlling foxes in such an environment becomes clearer: hills stretching for miles into the distance are smothered in an unrelenting carpet of dense timber. "This is tough country," Aled warns as hounds spread out to draw, "it's pointless racing around in here – you have to keep coming back to work the same patch of ground, and we find our pure Welsh hounds are best suited to the job." Meanwhile guns have lined forestry rides, and I walk into a stand of ancient conifers, whose trunks are wrapped in green shawls of damp moss to listen for the sound of hounds. A woodcock flits noiselessly between the trees, and a jay's harsh screech grates on the silence. Then I hear the tinkle of hound music, followed by the distant pop of gunfire.

I return to the ride for news of progress and find Mark Richards waiting beside his van; the Paxton's followers communicate in Welsh, so I am none the wiser when the agricultural contractor's two-way radio cackles, but Mark tells me two foxes have already been shot on the far side of the hill. Doreen Evans, whose father formed the Spitre Hunt back in the Fifties, drives up in a Land Rover, with the Master's daughter, Nerys, wearing a sweatshirt emblazoned in Welsh. When I ask her to translate, she tells me with a grin, "I may not be an angel, but I speak the language of heaven." Later I meet Arthur Higgins, a plumber from Warrington, who does not carry a gun, but enjoys hunting with this tight knit community. "My wife and I have been visiting for twenty years," he tells me, "we love it to bits, and the lads are a great bunch. I enjoy a drink with them afterwards, and of course the fishing is great – I got an 8lb sea trout in June."

The able deputy huntsman wades through waist high undergrowth all day, cheering hounds as only a Welshman can. Aled carries a stick instead of a gun but feels no remorse when a fox is shot down in front of his pack. "The farmers pay for the hunt's upkeep," he explains, "so we have to respect their wishes and shoot foxes, although the hounds kill about twenty percent on their own." From our vantage point on the brow of a hill, he gestures towards smallholdings lying between banks of woodland in a narrow green valley. "Last year one of those farmers lost over fifty lambs to foxes. This isn't sport, it's pest control."

As Simon Hart points out, that is the big difference between hunting in the Welsh uplands and lowland Britain. "In Wales the purpose of hunting is destruction, whereas in the shires it is managing a sustainable population," he says. "There are parts of Wales where it is difficult for traditional mounted hunting to make a significant impact on the fox population. Some of the uniquely large forestry blocks cannot be hunted effectively without the aid of guns, but deploying this method in more open country may not work, which is why a combination of different hunting techniques has evolved to the satisfaction of Welsh farmers." During the day I realised there was another difference between riding to hounds and hunting purely for control purposes – the fox is reduced from the elevated position of quarry species to the rank of mere vermin, and with that demotion goes the respect some of us have for his legendary cunning and bravery.

Whatever your own views, there is no doubting the Paxton's efficiency, or its determination to hunt in a responsible and well organised fashion. But for me the most rewarding moment was watching a pack of lovely Welsh hounds streaming across a rare stretch of open country having pushed their quarry away from the trees and rattled round in a big loop behind Brechfa village. For the final draw of the day, Aled crosses a valley where a cloud of mist is drifting like smoke from an autumn bonfire. Hounds are soon clamouring on the line of another fox, but when a shot rings out five minutes later the music goes out like a light, and the day is brought to a sudden close.

As many of the Paxton's followers are farmers who have to get home in time for milking, the hunt normally finishes well before nightfall, but it is dusk before we are back at the pub tucking into cawl – a hearty meat and vegetable broth – and discussing the day. Aled is delighted with the performance of the hounds, and with the tally of seven foxes killed. He and I hold different views on hunting with hounds, but when I thank my hosts for their hospitality and set off for the long drive home, I leave behind a special camaraderie in the warm pub, and a hunt that provides a necessary and much appreciated service to the local farming community.

Hunting's rallying cry

A day with the Duke of Beaufort's, November 2004

This was a most depressing occasion, however the hunt's determination to find a way forward shone through, and nearly twenty years later the Duke of Beaufort's continues to flourish. When Captain Ian Farquhar gave up carrying the horn Tony Holdsworth stepped into the breech as professional huntsman and was in turn succeeded by Matt Ramsden, who became the Joint Master and amateur huntsman in 2016. Charlie Dando and Rory Akerman both trained on as expected; as a hunting blacksmith Charlie whipped-in to Matt as an amateur and has recently moved to the Monmouthshire as Joint Master and huntsman. Rory enjoyed five seasons as professional huntsman to the Tiverton and is now back at Badminton helping his father on their estate farm and hunting on a regular basis.

I AM BEING driven to dinner by the Joint Master and huntsman of the Duke of Beaufort's hunt, Captain Ian Farquhar, when a fox steps onto the road with the easy nonchalance that comes from living as a privileged tenant in this

oft-hunted corner of Gloucestershire. The Captain slams on the brakes to
avoid knocking down a friend he may meet as his quarry on the hunting field
tomorrow, and as he stifles a whoop of excitement the words of the poet
Will Ogilvie flash suddenly before me, "Not for the hate of the hunted, we
English saddle and ride…." But there is little else to whoop about this dark
November night, for yesterday a seven-year battle of attrition was finally
lost when the Parliament Act was deployed to force through an outright ban
on hunting with dogs.

Sporting writers and artists may have favoured the Elysian Fields of
High Leicestershire when documenting the golden ages of foxhunting, but
the iconic surroundings of Badminton House and Park are unquestionably
the sport's spiritual home. It was to these kennels that the fifth Duke of
Beaufort returned in the mid-18th century having enjoyed such a good run
on a fox from Silk Wood that from that day on he abandoned the pursuit of
deer in favour of foxes — a policy sustained by his descendants right up to the
present day Duke, who like every other successor to the title has taken on
the mastership of his family pack. The ducal seat of Badminton has also stood
the test of time, the stately surroundings virtually unchanged for centuries,
whilst the hounds have for long been a valuable source of blood to breeders
all over the world looking to introduce size and style into their own kennels.

There is a sense of disbelief among the 200-odd riders and an even
greater number of foot followers assembled at the kennels for the meet
the next day, almost a stubborn refusal to recognise the brutal reality that
a conspiracy of malevolent backbenchers in the Palace of Westminster has
brought down the axe on their way of life — it is indeed hard to imagine that
such a gathering of law-abiding country people will be outlawed by the time
this article appears in print. Friends greet each other as if nothing sinister
has happened at all, hound breeding guru Martin Scott points out a favourite
bitch, and with the first flecks of snow swirling through leaden skies, the
whisper on everyone's lips is of an improved scent, a day when hounds will
run like smoke across the celebrated Beaufortshire turf. Only professional
hunt staff Tony Holdsworth and Paul Hardwick look as if they have been hit
by a sledgehammer between the eyes.

But when the Joint Master stands up in his stirrups to address the crowd
the silence is immediate and profound. Everyone is waiting to hear his
verdict on what the future holds; however, the man who has hunted hounds

four days a week for the last 30 seasons does not have the answer this time. But Captain Farquhar does have the foxhunter's irrepressible optimism, and the confidence of a natural leader. When he pledges the resolve of his Joint Master and chairman to find a way through, and promises, "there will always be hounds at Badminton, there will always be hunting at Badminton," the thunderous applause causes horses to pirouette on their heels, and the hounds to sing briefly in approval. Then the crowds part to let the cavalcade through, and moments later the bitches are racing across springy turf, hungry for the first fox of the day.

As the huge field follows, the famous Badminton herd of red deer bunch tightly in anxious formation, wet noses testing the winter morning as steam rises from a hundred wet backs to form a halo above a forest of majestic antlers. Against this backdrop Helen Rowe introduces herself with the words, "last week I chained myself to the Houses of Parliament," and I ponder the absurdity of a government that compels a vet from Tetbury to take such drastic action. Today's field is full of individuals who have played leading roles in the fight to save hunting, including Professor Roger Scruton, joint architect of a declaration that has over 40,000 signatories prepared to break the law – although enthusiasm for outright defiance now seems to be evaporating quicker than a vixen's scent.

Another is Lord Mancroft on a striking grey, looking drained and ashen after a week of political ping-pong between the two Houses. I ask him who is the worst, most bigoted, of all our opponents and he immediately answers, "Kaufman. He is vitriolic and full of hatred. I would like to see him tarred, feathered, and then dumped in a very public place." Mancroft's views will be shared by many whose lives will be shattered on February 18th. Last October the Master's daughter, this morning elegantly attired in the blue and buff livery worn by Beaufort subscribers, infiltrated the Labour Party conference with a group of friends. "Up until then I had no concept of the sheer hatred our opponents feel towards us; it was terrifying," Emma Wade tells me through chattering teeth. I am not sure if she is shivering at the memory of Brighton or the icy sleet soaking into her coat.

The Icehouse is blank, but hounds open in Allengrove, hesitantly at first, then with increased confidence, until the woodlands ring to the bitches' soprano voices. The electric twang of the huntsman's horn follows hard on the heels of David Hall's holloa, and as hounds stream away from covert the massed mounted field push and shove for a good start – this is the cut and thrust of foxhunting at its glamorous best, the excitement, the anticipation, and a hundred unanswered questions on the lips of every rider. But there is a sense of the anticlimax when the bitches are brought to their noses by soggy maize stubble within three fields and can only persevere as far as Cherry Orchard. The next fox leads us through Swangrove, magnificent woodland where broad avenues reach out from the centre like the limbs of a starfish. Over the years I have stood in the centre of this natural amphitheatre and watched countless foxes cross these hallowed rides.

Surrounded by grassland laced with thorn hedges, it is hard to imagine a more delectable setting for a fox covert than the next draw, Sopworth Break. Although there were foxes here during autumn hunting, this time rafts of warm laid thorn and thick briars fail to hold. But this is Beaufortshire, and drawing one cherished covert blank is no cause for despondency – there is always another just around the corner. The shoulder of the hill beside Widleys is carved into green chunks by a triple line of thick black hedges, and Bridget Cross, who has kindly provided the hunters for your correspondent to ride, warns me not to get in close to the middle one should hounds run that way. But the hunted fox denies us shivering survivors clasping wet reins with wet hands the thrill of the Widleys' hedges, and instead heads into the back of Sherston village, and the intervention of a fresh fox.

I had been told the previous evening about farmers' sons Charlie Dando and Rory Akerman, so have little difficulty in identifying Charlie when a grinning boy with a muddy back rides up and announces that he has just fallen off whilst jumping a fence for *The Field* photographer. After the hunt staff, it is his generation that will suffer most from the ban on hunting. As twelve-year-old Charlie will be too young to be arrested I suggest a cunning plan. "Excellent idea," he agrees enthusiastically, "I will carry the horn and Rory can be my whipper-in." That would be a fitting, if implausible, solution, for there cannot be another hunt supported by quite so many farmers and their families riding regularly to hounds.

It is late afternoon when hounds find in the Gun Club, which Peter Sidebottom tells me was blank last time as he gallops past, cramming down his hat in anticipation of a good evening run. Hounds settle to hunt as well as they have gone all day, but after crossing the main railwayline by a stone bridge the bitches are hit by electric fencing, and can only trickle slowly into Cranwell on a diminishing scent. All day I have watched in admiration as Chris Casey has given a faultless display of fieldmastering, never jumping a fence when hounds are not running, but tackling anything in his path during the course of a hunt. Here, as always, the highest standards have been maintained. But now dusk is gathering, and the frustrations of a poor scenting day prove too much for a couple of Beaufort ladies, who fly a stiff hedge as their Field Master leads his charges through an open gateway. But unlike the late Duke, who once sent my mother home for a similar offence, Chris smiles diplomatically and pretends not to notice.

Back at the kennels it would normally be time to ponder a difficult scenting day, but on this evening the chat amongst those thawing out inside Tony Holdsworth's cottage is dominated by the bleakest future hunting has ever faced, and the ways in which this historic hunt can survive until such time as the ban is repealed, a thread of hope to which everyone clings. Outright defiance of the law is not an option, but according to Captain Farquhar, neither is admission of defeat. "Everyone involved with the hunt, backed by the Duke and myself, is determined to keep things going at Badminton," he says. "There is a firm resolve to maintain hounds, staff and our very special relationship with the farmers. We will be running a legally watertight enterprise – of that there is no question, however we will also test the letter of the law in every possible way." I bid the Captain and his staff goodnight, and as I leave them discussing the way forward, have the utmost confidence that in the difficult times ahead, the Duke of Beaufort's Hunt will continue to set an example for all others to follow.

Waggie, the tale of a huntsman's mare

A diminutive hunter's journey from the bogs of Dartmoor to High Leicestershire

If we are granted one horse of a lifetime, Waggie was mine.

I FIRST NOTICED her high up on Dartmoor during a November afternoon hunt in the late Eighties. Hounds had been running for the best part of an hour, across a landscape of quaking bogs and steep hillsides littered with grey splinters of broken granite. I remember my tired thoroughbred toiling up the slopes of Great Mis Tor as the pack disappeared over the fog-shrouded summit – and then a small bay mare racing past me and skipping over those jagged rocks hard-held on a tight rein. I did not see Waggie again that winter, for the word was that her owner had grown tired of battling with a mare determined to be in front of hounds, and preferably the fox as well. But our paths crossed a year later, towards the end of a long day hunting hounds on racehorses provided by a trainer whose greatest pleasure was a foray to Ascot sales to purchase other people's rejects.

Although my friend produced a fine steeplechaser for the meet that morning, by late afternoon I was on board a horse with withers marginally thicker than a razor blade, balanced on a racing plate so tiny that even the hounds threw me disparaging glances, never mind the bemused members of a depleted field. Just when I was considering blowing for home up rode Waggie's owner with a sympathetic smile. "My little mare is in the field if you want her," she offered. Fifteen minutes later I was presented with what appeared to be a very muddy and shaggy pony, but when we trotted off with the pack clustered around her heels, Waggie's big brown ears pricked forward to attention, and I felt her quick, extravagant stride flowing easily beneath me. She never moved a muscle as hounds fanned out to draw a kale field, but trembled with excitement when their cry stirred the winter's afternoon. The ensuing hunt may have been short, but my new conveyance did not squander a yard as she galloped after the pack, flying three wooden gates with disdainful ease.

Waggie's owners called to collect her that night, but I had spent long enough on her back to realise this was one horse I should not surrender without a struggle. Leaving my visitors inside the huntsman's cottage with a bottle of scotch, I tramped through driving rain to the flesh house where the hide man had left a bundle of notes beneath a blood-stained bucket, payment for skins pulled from the carcasses of Dartmoor's fallen stock over the past six weeks. By the time the whisky bottle was empty, a grubby brown envelope had been exchanged for the 15.2hh mealy-nosed mare. Later that week her passport dropped through the letterbox; it revealed that my new horse was already twelve years old, out of a mare called Dame Wagtail, but by a sire of pedigree unknown.

In conventional hunting countries subscribers enjoy adrenaline-packed days attacking hedges in the vale, but the holy grail for followers of the Spooners pack has always been Dartmoor's wide open spaces – a forbidding landscape, requiring no less skill to cross. The consequences of getting stogged – Devon vernacular for sinking into a bottomless hole in the peat

– are dire, and trying to extricate an exhausted horse from a pit of freezing slime miles from any road is not an experience for the faint-hearted. But the chances of such a fate aboard Waggie were almost non-existent. Here was a horse that never missed her turn, jumped like a stag, and could almost walk on water. Time after time that season she skimmed like a water boatman across swamps that would have drowned other horses in minutes, and at meets I began to notice even the hardiest subscribers looking a little concerned when they saw their huntsman mounted on Waggie for a day on the moor.

Fur Tor lies at the peaty heart of Dartmoor, a weather-beaten bulb of granite protruding from treacherous quagmires, a place so remote that it enjoys a reputation steeped in mystery and legend. The rocks littering its slopes are a favoured refuge for Dartmoor foxes, but there are few ways of reaching Fur Tor on horseback; they all require nerves of steel. One approach is to follow the stream bed of the Amicombe brook; another is along a pass cut through peat in medieval times so that men living at the heart of the moor could carry their dead to Lydford on the western fringe for burial. The cutting has been neglected for decades, and is now barely navigable, the narrow black walls scarred by the passage of countless stirrups through the years. Seasons can pass without a ridden horse setting foot on Fur Tor, but Waggie came to know it well, and I have the brush of a fox pulled down amongst the boulders at dusk to remind me of those desolate surroundings.

When the time came to decide which horses to take north to my new hunt, Waggie was not top of the list. How could a moorland pony be expected to cope with the cut and thrust of the Sinnington vale? She may have walked across water on Dartmoor, but Yorkshire's greasy fields of plough would surely wrench legs that peat and bog had failed to anchor. But when the lorry set off on the long journey north, Waggie was on board. She had once performed with distinction at moonlight steeplechases in Devon, informal races run in stubble fields after harvest, and before leaving Dartmoor competed in one last contest of another kind – a cross-country race over stone walls, bogs and rivers organised by a neighbouring hunt. Waggie galloped round so quickly that some of her rivals had not reached the halfway stage as she crossed the finishing line a distance in front.

Killing four foxes from her back on the first morning's hunting in Yorkshire was surely a good omen, but I never imagined the mare would not only complete her first season there, but many more to follow. Thumbing through the pages of my hunting diaries is like taking a journey back in time, as memories of great hunts of the past come flooding back – points of five, six and seven miles, and on 22nd January 1994, one of the four truly great hunts it has been my privilege to witness; a sixteen-mile run in the hill country that finished miles beyond our hunt boundary in Farndale. That night I wrote in my hunting diary, "luckily I was riding my terrifically game and clever little mare, without whom I could never have stayed in touch over the wettest moorland." Years later the Farndale keeper told me he had fished our fox's carcass out of the River Dove, long after the leading hounds had done their work.

The Sinnington hold at least four hunt balls every winter; parties where hard-drinking gamekeepers, farmers and locals shake village halls to the rafters, only pausing to feast from a groaning buffet prepared by their wives. Late one such evening, the hunt chairman and I struck a wager – to win I had to leave his lawn meet in eight hours' time straight over the ha-ha, and not down the gravelled driveway as usual. Not for the first time, Waggie came to the rescue, and the chairman's cash was mine. When the Sinnington met at another fine manor house after an absence of several years, the mare played her part in making a piece of history. Well lubricated by our host's lethal Percy Specials, I remember popping Waggie over some rails into a new plantation and all but landing on a dozing fox. There were smiles all round when the right conclusion was reached thirty minutes later and racehorse trainer Peter Easterby declared with a grin, "that's the end of the Cold War" – a reference to the owner's reconciliation with the hunt, and from that day on, the name of the covert where the fox was found.

After eight seasons in Yorkshire, and at twenty years of age, Waggie had earned semi-retirement, and the chance to procreate. The services of a stallion were exchanged for a haunch of venison – but despite the owner's reputation for being able to get any mare in foal, Waggie remained stubbornly immune to his magic. She spent most of the following winter on loan to a hunting-mad teenager but proved she had lost none of her sparkle when bolting with the girl's mother down Sutton Bank, one of Yorkshire's longest and steepest hills. The little mare looked so pleased with herself after that incident that she was reclaimed for the whipper-in to ride during spring hunting. When the time came for a move to the glamorous environs of the Quorn and high Leicestershire, this time there was no agonising over Waggie's fate. To leave her behind was unthinkable.

If killing four foxes in Yorkshire had been a good omen, pulling out lame for her first morning in Leicesteshire was the opposite, although Waggie came sound enough to hunt her third pack of hounds in a strangely familiar landscape – the bracken, rocks and hills of the Quorn Tuesday country in Charnwood Forest. But age was catching up with her fast, and after one season with the Quorn she moved to the Johnson family at Quenby Lodge. Here Ginny – who was once placed third at Badminton – cared for her as only someone born and bred amongst horses, hounds and dogs is able. Lavished with TLC, and stuffed with drugs and potions of every description, the old mare was kept sound enough for the odd stolen hour in the hunting field.

But now the family's impending move has compelled me once again to consider her future. During the past weeks I have often contemplated the final words of an Australian poem by Banjo Paterson, "*I dare not ride him for fear he'd fall, But he does a journey to beat them all, For though he scarcely a trot can raise, He takes me back to the droving days.*" But this is England, with her cruel, cold winters to accentuate the pain of tired limbs and aching joints, and the kindest road is the one down which countless great hunters of the past have travelled. The huntsman's merciful bullet, delivered in the familiar surroundings of home, and immortality through the flesh and blood of a pack of foxhounds.

For how long can Exmoor's deer survive the ban?

A day with the Devon and Somerset Staghounds, March 2005

For several years Tom Yandle — whom I had first met on a Yorkshire grouse moor — was kind enough to invite me to stay for a week in March to "keep the hunters fit for Easter" whilst he was preoccupied with lambing. The Yandle horses were perhaps the fittest and best conveyances on Exmoor and the Staghounds' huntsman, Donald Summersgill, showed fine sport and invariably accounted for his quarry. The day described below was one of my first outings with a mounted pack after the Hunting Act had become law and it all felt desperately strange. Thankfully Tom's worst fears have not been realised, for although there are now alternative methods of control in place, the Devon and Somerset Staghounds still play an important role in the management of Exmoor's wild red deer.

I AM SITTING astride one of Tom Yandle's clever Exmoor hunters watching a line of wild red deer moving in single file up a headland on the opposite side of a coombe. There are two spring stags amongst the hinds, and even though my vantage point on the cusp of Winsford punchbowl is more than half a mile away, it is obvious the deer are unperturbed by the presence of riders in the valley beneath them. A stiff breeze is sweeping cloud shadows across the green patchwork of fields stretching uphill towards the darker bulk of Dunkery Beacon, the rocks on her summit sparkling briefly when a shaft of sunlight pierces the clouds. I can hear lambs bleating from pastures enclosed by stone-faced banks, and the shrill chortle of an unseen cock pheasant, but another sound I have always associated with spring on Exmoor is strangely absent.

Soon after the deer have melted into the landscape a single hound appears on their trail, but although I strain my ears, I cannot hear a note of hound music above gusts of wind buffeting banks of brown heather on the brow of Winsford Hill. Unlike the deer he is pursuing, General appears hesitant, even bemused, by the absence of his comrades – but he is visibly invigorated when another hound appears, and together they resume pursuit, tracing the line beneath whitewashed farmhouses on the far side of the valley. But a hunt without music is like a film without words; only by extreme concentration and a great deal of luck is it possible to follow the plot. Welcome to Tony Blair's Exmoor, where the famous Devon and Somerset Staghounds have been reduced to managing the deer they have safeguarded for the last 150 years with just two hounds.

Talk to any knowledgeable supporter of the Staghounds and you will come away convinced that the hunt's overriding priority has always been the long-term future of Exmoor's red deer herd. Tom Yandle, a working farmer who has been chairman of this hunt since 1996, articulates the complex and now increasingly fragile relationship between the deer, the farmers and the hunt. "We have approximately 5,000 deer living in the counties of Devon and Somerset, which is equal to the total population for the rest of England and Wales combined," he explains as we watch the huntsman encourage his hounds at the head of Little Ash Coombe. "That is largely thanks to the way they have been managed by the three packs of staghounds hunting the region. Although farmers have the legal right to shoot deer on their own land, the vast majority refrain from doing so as the deer are regarded as the property of the community, and their management is left with absolute confidence to the hunt." The farmer's role as host to the hunt and custodian of its quarry is reciprocated by the hunt in different ways – many farmers enjoy following the hunt in vehicles or on horseback, and after a deer has been killed the venison is distributed amongst those who farm the area in which it was found.

Hunting an artificial drag was never an option for this hunt's Joint Masters, Diana and Maurice Scott, and George Witheridge whose subscribers hunt primarily to watch hounds at work, not jump fences. "We were determined not to do anything artificial, but to carry on hunting as best as possible within the new law," Diana Scott explains. "We all care for the deer too much to hand over their management to someone else; we just had to continue, however difficult that proves to be." Diana's reference to deer management extends beyond the 100 selectively culled each year by the hunt – an equal number are humanely dispatched behind the scenes by the hunt staff, whom are on call 24 hours a day, seven days a week, to deal with sick or wounded deer reported by members of the public.

But deer hit by speeding motorists do not wait conveniently in the bushes to be shot. Despite the often appalling nature of their injuries they do everything possible to avoid capture, even though death from starvation or loss of blood will inevitably follow. By preventing hunts from using a sensible number of hounds in these situations, the Hunting Act prolongs the suffering of the animal it purports to protect. "The law still permits just two hounds even if their purpose is to help dispatch a wounded deer," Tom Yandle explains, "it would be much more humane to use several hounds, which would locate the deer quicker and easier. Stalkers are reputed to have specially trained dogs, but no one has seen them down here – our hounds are definitely the best way of dealing with this problem."

The hunt continued to honour its commitment to go out three times a week until the end of the season, with at least two people in addition to the hunt staff carrying a specially adapted shotgun with which to shoot the stag at close range. Deer have always been dispatched in this manner, however the fundamental difference is that before February 18th the hunted stag was shot only when it stood at bay, having been given every opportunity to evade capture after fair pursuit that favoured survival of the fittest. To comply with the new legislation the hunt now intends to shoot the chosen stag as soon as possible after it has been flushed.

The difficulties of ambushing fresh deer in this way are considerable, and according to Tom Yandle, "on some days this happens quickly, and on others it may not take place until late afternoon, if at all." If the stag continues to evade the guns, the result may be a succession of aborted flushes spread over many miles, during which the original two hounds are substituted for a fresh couple whenever the opportunity arises, sometimes providing spectators and followers with the type of hunting run that was normal before the new law came into force. "Alun Michael and his cronies are always asking us why we don't just shoot the stag when it is selected by the harbourer," Tom continues, "but it's not as simple as that. It may have been spotted through binoculars from the other side of a valley among a large group of other deer. The chosen stag must be flushed out in order to be shot."

However on this day things do not go according to plan and our stag mysteriously vanishes after an hour's pursuit. One or two of the foot followers claim to have seen him creep into the side of a small coombe, but despite the huntsman taking to his feet and conducting a thorough search, there is no trace to be found. For Donald Summersgill, who has carried the horn here for the last fourteen seasons, the frustrations of performing an already difficult task with just two hounds must be immense, but he is equally concerned about the other members of the pack languishing in kennels whilst a fortunate few perform the role for which they were bred. "I am using a nucleus of just five hounds from a working pack of over thirty couple," he tells me. We avoid an unpalatable discussion over the destiny of the redundant workers, but unless something changes, their fate is surely sealed.

Although the appeal to mounted followers has been diminished by the new law, the hunt has continued to enjoy the support of locals and visitors alike, including hunt president Dick Lloyd wearing his trademark moss green bowler hat, who describes a recent day following his eightieth birthday meet in glowing terms. When I ask another long-standing lady subscriber if she has been hunting regularly since the ban she replies tactfully, "well, let's say I have been coming out." John Dorse visiting from the Taunton Vale answers the same question in a similar vein; "it's not quite the same as hunting, but we must support them."

By 2.30pm our day is over, but driving home in the lorry we encounter a group of vehicles parked up at Mounsey Hill Gate. Tom winds down the window to find out what is going on and is informed by a grinning countryman, "rabbiting." Strangely enough the pursuit of rabbits with as many dogs as you wish is still a lawful activity. Myself, Tom and American writer PJ O'Rourke – here to report on the madness that is England under New Labour – stride out across the gorse-flecked moorland, and presently an extra-large rabbit comes loping past, with the merry music of beagles ringing in her wake. Even the most determined efforts of New Labour cannot suppress the humour of the Exmoor hunting community and when we catch up with the beagles' lean Master he says to Tom, "I tell 'ee what, I'll lend 'ee a couple of my beagles to hunt your stags – two hounds 'aint enough for that job. We could tell 'em we were re-training to hunt rabbits."

Much has been written elsewhere about the cosy kitchen at Riphay Barton, where Mrs Yandle provides constant sustenance to an endless stream of visitors. Farm hands with accents as thick as clotted cream, teenage students, and tweedy hunting visitors from up country are all welcomed here as equals. A kettle simmers permanently on the range, and the mantelpiece above is crammed with faded bowlers, old hunting photographs, and antlers from great hunts of the past. It is here that Tom reveals his concerns for the future of his hunt, and the red deer of Exmoor. "It remains to be seen if using hounds to control deer within the law is going to work long term. What is important is not how we kill the deer, but how we prevent them from being killed. At the moment farmers are still leaving that job to us, but once one starts to shoot deer his neighbours will follow suit, and if the deer were managed by DEFRA or the National Park Authority the farmers would do exactly as they pleased. I would not be the least surprised if by next Christmas the deer were starting to get shot. Why should farmers preserve them if all we are allowed to do is muck around with two hounds?"

Once more into the ditches

A day with the Meath in Ireland, November 2006

When hunting hounds, I had always planned to visit Ireland in the event of a freeze-up England, but somehow it never happened and this day with the Meath remains the only time I have hunted in the Emerald Isle. I flew to Dublin expecting to follow hounds on a wing and prayer, however the Meath were well organised and careful to avoid damaging farmland in wet conditions. The unusual arrangement — possibly unique — whereby the Henry brothers took it in turns to hunt hounds as a professional one day and Field Master the next appeared to work well, however I doubt it would have been acceptable on my side of the Irish Sea.

FORMER CHIEF EXECUTIVE of the Countryside Alliance and famous explorer, Robin Hanbury-Tenison, told me a story of how he was put on the spot at a Countryside Alliance meeting attended by the most senior foxhunters in the land. "If you care so much about hunting, why don't you hunt yourself?" demanded an indignant heckler. Quick as lightning, Robin replied "because I grew up in Ireland and once you have hunted there you never want to hunt anywhere else." That response may have silenced the critic, but it is a sentiment I have heard expressed many times elsewhere, although the eulogies to Irish hunting are increasingly tempered with references to the problems rumoured to beset modern-day hunting over the water, including development, mains electric fencing, and unsympathetic farmers.

Being dispatched by the Editor to go and find out for myself during a day's hunting with any pack I wished sounded like a dream assignment, but the difficulty for someone who has visited Ireland only to judge hounds in summer is knowing which to choose. The old cliché *kid in a sweet shop* sprang to mind as I grappled with the options. Should it be the banks of County Limerick and a stay at the legendary Dunraven Arms, the chance to gallop over the Galway Blazers' stone walls and grassland that, according to Snaffles, would make me "say sick wi' leppin" or perhaps the black and tan hounds of the Scarteen, now hunted by Chris Ryan, whose family have been Masters of the unique pack for over three hundred years. In the end I telephoned the former Master of the Meath hunt, the delightful Penny Lindsay-Fynn, and took up her long-standing invitation to come and stay for a hunt.

As a result, I find myself at a meet of this famous pack on the third Friday in November, chatting to their assistant Secretary, Henry Reeves, who is recovering from a replacement hip operation, but does not anticipate returning to the saddle. "The ditches are big around here you know," he tells me completely straight-faced, "you need to be pretty agile to get out of one." Looking around I recognise Norman Williamson, whom I had last met during my time as Joint Master and huntsman of the Quorn. I remember remonstrating with Norman after he had treated the field to a flawless but wholly unnecessary display of horsemanship involving a line of fences near Gaddesby, and now rather wish I had stayed silent – there is something of the "we'll show you today mister" in the ex-National Hunt jockey's firm handshake when we renew acquaintanceship. Visitors from England include Katie Dashwood, who arrived in time for breakfast having caught the night ferry, and Richard de Courcy who normally hunts with the Berkeley.

Ten minutes later, I am one of nearly 90 riders jostling impatiently like cattle in the corner of a grass field. As only the hunt staff and Masters are wearing scarlet I am thankful for the loan of a black Lindsay-Fynn coat, and Penny's wise counsel against wearing a red one. But where is the famous Irish craic? Covertside chatter is strangely absent, and when the suspense proves too much for some the offenders are ruthlessly silenced by the Field Master, Kenny Henry, who rises in his stirrups as hounds open in Churchtown. "Lads," he shouts, the single word slicing like a butcher's knife through the winter morning. "You all know the craic – no talking. And keep to the headlands today, it's very wet." The field cowers in obedient silence and although Churchtown is but a silhouette in the distance, we can hear hounds hunting merrily, followed by a long thrilling holloa to signal the fox away.

Ireland is celebrated for the quality of her hirelings, and from the start – skittering down the ramp all gloss and quality on dancing hoof beats – Trap 6 does not disappoint. We scurry across a rough and unkempt country that screams *fox, fox, fox* from every bog-green blade of grass – a landscape of full ditches and wet, low-lying pastures spiked with rushes the colour of hedgehog spines. We gallop past skeletal trees lying where they have fallen on the sodden turf and bound over ditches as deep as mine shafts. There is a knack to crossing this country, which includes riding cautiously through gateways so deep and boggy they would topple an elephant going any quicker than a walk. There is usually only one way in and out of each small enclosure and I try to heed the warning offered by Johnny Vance, a visiting Joint Master of the Fermanagh Harriers, to keep within the leading half dozen or risk seeing nothing of the action.

When hounds run their fox to ground after a short hunt the ear-ringed Dermot Ryan – described by one member of the hunt as someone who "clips his horses but not himself" – seeks me out to check I am happy with his horse and the answer is a resounding yes. As hounds draw on, I meet the immaculately attired Peter Newell, who is a grandson of the famous Ikey Bell. Dressed in buff cord breeches, garter straps, beautifully tied stock and wearing a black coat set off by a silk topper, Peter's elegant profile could have been lifted straight from the canvas of a Lionel Edwards painting. His cut-glass English accent is markedly different from the soft Irish brogue of his fellow subscribers but attracts no comment or resentment. Irish hunts have a long history of welcoming English and American visitors, sometimes inviting them to form masterships with the locals. Understandably, the Westminster ban raised concerns of an English invasion – now largely academic as hunts back home continue to thrive through a combination of enterprise, determination and resilience. However, not one person I met during my stay in Ireland would have disagreed with Vance's summary – "the visitors we get from England are very welcome and we like to see them, but a mass migration would never be acceptable."

When we have to negotiate a particularly hairy crossing a classic scene unfolds to the backdrop of a bemused sheep wandering belly deep in ditch water. First, live electric wire is secured, and then riders take their turn to slide down what resembles a muddy ski run, pick their way along the riverbed and scramble up a glass-smooth bank. The huntsman's son, ten-year-old Evan Henry, mounted on a smart grey pony, is one of the first to cross, but several riders, including Joint Master Ben Dillon, are knocked from their horses by a thick branch waiting like an executioner for victims. Dillon's hat is fished from the water by a gallant follower, the sheep rescued, and the hunt continues on its way – and hounds are not even running. "I get permission to have the day off school," Evan tells me when I join him on the far bank, "my teacher is into hunting as well."

Most farms in Ireland run to less than a hundred acres, and big estates are rare. This presents an onerous burden on the mastership preparing country for a day's hunting, and many hunts rely on their staff for assistance. This is the case at the Meath where two brothers uniquely share both the horn and field mastering duties. Professional John Henry hunts the bitches on Mondays and Fridays, whilst his brother Kenny controls the field, with a role reversal on Wednesdays when the doghounds are out. According to Joint Master, Andrew Boyd, "John Henry knows the country so well that he almost thinks like a fox." Both huntsmen are assisted by professional whipper-in Mark Casserly, referred to as Spud, and the honorary whipper-in Aidan Galligan.

There is a cold nip in the air for the final hunt of the day and the pack's cry resonates with the special, spine-tingling note that seems reserved for the onset of dusk – but hounds are stopped when the fox heads back into country we have already covered. With the bitches safely loaded I have the chance to discuss hounds and hunting with John Henry, who is articulate, friendly and welcoming. The Meath have used stallion hounds from the Cheshire and Beaufort and I am handed a marked meet card together with an invitation to return. "Not a week passes that we don't have English visitors,"

John tells me, "you've been unlucky today as I was looking for a quiet one with so many people out. No one ever goes home early here; their motto is: "Don't leave until you see the hounds in the truck." The elusive craic now kicks in at the local pub, where landlords Leo and Carmel Geraghty produce sandwiches and serve riders Guinness and hot whiskey.

The following day we attend the meet of the Westmeath on foot, where their whipper-in Noel Murphy sings the praises of a Sinnington draft whose parents I bred. We join locals on a hilltop overlooking a ravishing vista of grassland bathed in winter sunshine – the Elysian scene completed by a fox stealing away in full view of the spectators, but when I hear a horn clearly not blown by the huntsman, my first reaction is that the antis have arrived. However, "gone away" is the ring tone on Kevin Maguire's mobile. After he reveals the fate that befell the last group of saboteurs to have visited his hunt I form the impression that antis are one category of tourist well advised to stick to the English side of the Irish Sea.

I half-expected to meet foxhunters who had emigrated to Ireland to avoid the ban in England, but even if they do exist, none was forthcoming. Instead I tracked down Warwickshire landowner, Philip Shirley, who does the next best thing and flies out to hunt with the Louth regularly during the season. "I fly over about once a week, get met on arrival and driven straight to the meet," he says. "Last Saturday I even got back to England in time to go out to dinner." In case anyone thinks that this sounds like a good idea, Philip points out that as a landowner in the Louth country, he is uniquely placed to visit. "I am not sure anyone else would be allowed to hunt as often as I do," he admits, "even if they were mad enough to want to."

In fact, Edward Mahony combines running Tattersalls in Newmarket with being Master of the Louth, and Philip's wife, Augusta, has also tried commuting, although she found the travelling exhausting. "The final straw was being forced to take off my hunting boots every time I went through departures," she recalls. "I love the people, and the wild country, which can be terrifying to cross when hounds really run, but you have to be lucky – there is nothing to beat a good day in Ireland but in England sport is often better organised and therefore more predictable." And that is my verdict based on my short visit to the Emerald Isle – strike it lucky in a good bit of country with a small field and you may experience the hunt of a lifetime. But be prepared for some frustrating days before the red-letter one of your dreams comes along, and when it does, don't entertain ideas of hunting in Ireland permanently – an English hunting visitor is one thing, an immigrant quite another.

Keepers game for the hunt

Hunting and shooting working together in North Yorkshire, March 2011

Les Green

Hunting enthusiasts in North Yorkshire are fortunate that so many shooting estates, together with the gamekeepers that work for them, extend such a warm welcome to hounds. This is thanks in no small part to the legacy of sporting landowners, and a love of venery passed down through generations of local gamekeeping families. There is no finer example of the modern sporting squire than George Winn-Darley, a keen shot who also rides regularly to hounds, especially when the Middleton or Sinnington Hunts are on his own land. George's former headkeeper at Aldby, Les Green, is sadly no longer with us, but his fondness for all field sports and determination that hunting and shooting must get along is mirrored across much of North Yorkshire today.

IT'S THE FIRST Thursday in March in Winn-Darley country – a land of corn, woodland and pasture divided by the River Derwent in her middle reaches and presided over by the magnificent Aldby Park. A life-size portrait of the Darley Arabian – one of three Arab stallions from which all modern thoroughbreds trace their descent – hangs in the grand hallway, although there is nothing pretentious about the house's owner, George Winn-Darley. Barely a month has passed since I sat down to an end of season shoot lunch here with locals, friends and gamekeepers, amongst them the Aldby headkeeper and passionate hunting man, Les Green. Les had confirmed the date for his annual gamekeepers' meet with the Middleton hunt, together with a promise that at least four of his colleagues from around the county would attend on the back of a horse.

The day gets off to an inauspicious start when the hunt lorry pulls up in a lay-by, and out jumps the second whipper-in, Joss Bentley, white as a sheet. He shuffles into a corner and fumbles ineffectively with his breeches before turning to the young Joint Master, Tom Holt, and asking; "please sir, can you give me a hand?" Joss slammed his fingers in a kennels door that morning, but despite the acute discomfort he has no intention of missing the meet at Les and Jo Green's cottage overlooking the Derwent, where several keepers are already making light work of their host's whisky. I recognise several familiar faces amongst those dressed in tweed but on two legs, including Andrew Lander and Ted and Alan Wass from the Sinnington country, whilst the home pack is represented by keepers from Birdsall, Garrowby, Lowthorpe, Huttons Ambo, Upper Helmsley, Raisthorpe and Sledmere estates.

This keepers' day is particularly important for Tom Holt, who at 24 years old is the youngest of the Middleton's six Joint Masters by some way, but also the one responsible for arranging most of the hunting. His reward is to share carrying the horn with the hunt's experienced professional, Peter McColgan, who is in his eleventh season at Birdsall. Having been brought up in Sinnington Hunt country at the sporting Ravenswick estate some twenty miles the other side of Ryedale, Tom understands only too well the need to foster good relationships between hunting and shooting. "There aren't very many ways you can show your appreciation and say thank you in hunting, but this is one of them," he says. "We would like as many keepers out mounted as possible, but above all it's a sociable day with hunters and shooters mucking in and having fun – the hunting is normally steady enough for everyone to stay in touch with the action."

Famous last words, for the pace was destined to be so quick on this mild day that the meet proved to be the only real opportunity for the exchange of gossip and chat. I had expected to find headkeepers Richard Hoggard and Trevor Ireland from Birdsall and Lowthorpe estates respectively amongst the mounted field but was surprised when the 2008 Gamekeeper of the Year, George Thompson, joined them and Les Green astride an unclipped and ancient conveyance. "I'm alright on four wheels with a drop of petrol but no good on hooves," he grinned with clenched teeth, "I feel very high, very dangerous and very unprotected." His appearance has earned the Spaunton grouse moor keeper a donation for his cancer charity fund. "Tom Holt pledged £50 if I turned up mounted today," he chuckles, "we've now raised over 30 grand." George Winn-Darley, who also owns Spaunton grouse moor, is looking on approvingly, although the joke doing the rounds at the meet is that his keeper has been instructed to return to his duties as soon as he has been snapped by the photographer.

A quick start to the day takes everyone by surprise, for hounds race away from a cover crop within minutes of moving off from the meet and leaving Scrayingham village on their left, swing round into Buttercrambe Thorns and on towards the cream of the Middleton country. We had expected a quiet day, but 40 minutes into this run regular subscribers are beaming with the satisfaction of being in on the sort of action normally reserved for the best of the hunt's Saturdays. There is no sign of George Thompson up front, so perhaps he has gone heather burning after all (in fact he endured another two hours before riding back to Aldby and tumbling off whilst trying to dismount), but Richard Hoggard is having a whale of a time. "Two jumps!" he yells as we clatter over a rare tarmac road on this busy, rollicking run; he later rides upsides and says with a big grin; "I hope I don't get a third one tonight, I'm knackered already." We all enjoy this sort of craic on the keepers' day, but with this pace the witty one liners are few and far between.

By now the pain of a broken finger is proving unbearable for Joss. On spotting Andy Hall, a Garrowby beatkeeper, he leaps off his horse and cajoles him to take his place. "I've not ridden since a kid, it feels a bit weird," says the man whose job is to help show some of the highest pheasants in the land for the hunt's chairman, the Earl of Halifax, as he pulls hastily requisitioned leggings on over Garrowby tweed. Field Master, John Cottingham, is keeping his charges in close touch with the action, but as we pop a set of rails onto a roadside verge ten minutes later a riderless horse comes galloping past, stirrups flailing against an empty saddle. A kind soul turns back to help Andy, and then Les Green is suddenly riding beside me. "Yer man wants a photo of me going over a jump but if he's not there I can't help him," he reasons. Ah yes, that must have been the photographer with his arms stretched wide in complaint half a mile back, but on days like this it's each man to his own, and devil take the hindmost.

Still the hunt continues. A six-bar iron gate sorts the men from the boys at the back of Skirpenbeck village and is quickly followed by a line of straggly bullfinches, one of which claims Kate Rangeley as a victim. "Don't worry, I'll be home to do the school run" she grins, clambering back into the saddle. Not usually one to leave the ground unnecessarily, George Winn-Darley rams his hireling at the thorns and is rewarded by a cheer as his mount sails over the obstacle. By mid-afternoon we are back in Lawson's Thorns, having spent most of the day on Aldby, which along with Joint Master, Michael Willoughby's Birdsall and the chairman's Garrowby, forms a golden triangle of delectable hunting country that is also home to some seriously good shooting. Les Green trots past on his weary horse whilst the pack rattle round this covert looking as happy as any keeper would at the end of a record-breaking day. "I am off on a bit further," he mutters, "there's no point being where the fish ain't."

Moments later Tom is blowing hounds away as they swoop across fields of pasture towards Garrowby. How appropriate on a day devoted to fostering relations between hunting and shooting, that hounds should run through the heart of this celebrated sporting estate. It has been a pleasure to see Tom handling them quietly and effectively all day, but despite his best efforts the line fizzles out above Uncleby as clay turns to chalk on the edge of the wolds. Being some way out of the draw and late on in the afternoon, Tom blows for home to conclude a virtuoso performance from hounds, huntsman and staff. Sean Edwards, the Garrowby head forester, has ridden with us throughout, and we follow him through the gloaming into his yard at Pasture Farm, where three generations of the Edwards family comprising former Middleton huntsman, Tony, and his grandchildren Carrie and Dan, dispense hospitality to the few remaining riders.

Scenting whisky and sandwiches from afar, several gamekeepers drop out of the sky like hawks, amongst them Andy Hall, none the worse for his tumble. Tom offers him another horse any day he wants. "Thanks very much, but once a year is enough for me," the keeper replies to peals of laughter, "but it's been brilliant. I shut my eyes over that first jump and when I opened them my feet were out the stirrups, and I was on my horse's backside – I just fell out the side door. Thanks a lot for that," he says, turning to Joss, "do let me shake your hand." The second whipper-in steps back smartly to more laughter, cradling his broken fingers. "Fat bastard," he jokes, handing back the keeper's tweed coat with his good hand, "I can fit two of me into that."

The banter continues until the hunt lorry arrives, and with horses and hounds loaded up it's time to go home. I hitch a lift back to my car with the Sledmere headkeeper, Derek Sanderson, and the chat during that short journey is all about what hunting is left for the current season. It is clear those days will be well attended by many of the keepers who work within the Middleton's expansive country, although few will be contemplating a return to four legs for at least another year. "I'm capped with it," Les Green says when I telephone to thank him for the ninth day's hunting he has provided at Aldby so far this season. "Hunting and shooting have got to work together, and we've shown them how to do that today."

Riding the high moor
A day with the Mid Devon, March 2019

I am writing this beneath a charming hand-painted menu that the Two Bridges Hunt Club kindly gave me after I addressed them as guest speaker during the evening described below. One of the great pleasures in hunting across Dartmoor is how little the landscape has changed over the years, with the exception of an alarming increase of gorse that is now threatening to engulf large tracts of former white grass and heather. For true lovers of venery there are few better settings in which to watch hounds work, whilst the challenges of staying in touch on horseback across often treacherous and tiring ground cannot be overstated. Unlike up country, there is never a moment to stand still when hunting the high moor.

FOUNDED BY THE Dartmoor hunting community in 1929 to reciprocate Edward, Prince of Wales's hospitality at nearby Prince Hall, the Two Bridges

Hunt Club has grown into something of institution for those who ride to hounds on Dartmoor. The club takes its name from a moorland outpost that stands beside the old turnpike road downstream of the West Dart's confluence with the River Cowsic. Membership is limited to a hundred individuals, drawn from subscribers to the four moorland packs that hunt the 450 square miles of high, wild country between Okehampton in the north and Ivybridge in the south, together with members of the Royal Navy Saddle Club, but all must be (or perhaps must have been) capable of 'riding the high moor.' This qualification may sound innocuous, but it takes a special skill to keep in touch with hounds when they race across terrain strewn with lumps of broken granite and quaking peat bogs.

Members meet up in February for dinner at the eponymous hotel, which is followed by a day's hunting provided in rotation by the Dartmoor, Mid Devon, South Devon, and Spooners & West Dartmoor Hunts. Thirty years have elapsed since I last donned hunt evening dress to attend the annual dinner – on that occasion I had to keep a clear head since it was my turn to provide sport the next day as Master and huntsman to the Spooners – this time I was returning by invitation of the chairman and former Mid Devon MFH, George Lyon-Smith, to propose the traditional toast to foxhunting after a fine dinner of locally raised beef. It was heartening to note the continued observance of other customs such as the signing of a record book by everyone present (each member is encouraged to invite a guest) and a raffle for the hand-painted menu cards that adorn every table. These charming depictions of hunting scenes and Dartmoor landmarks are contributed by local artists, which once included the famous equine and sporting painter Sir Alfred Munnings.

Another custom – and a concession to overindulgence the night before – is a delayed meet at 11.30am the following morning, which was well attended by hunting enthusiasts from all over Dartmoor. It had been the turn of the Spooners' hounds to perform this year, but as their Master, Andrew Smith, revealed to dinner guests the previous evening his hounds were coughing and unable to fulfil the obligation. Their place was taken by fifteen couple of sharp-looking hounds from the Mid Devon and their huntsman since 2016, Duncan Hume MFH, who graduated to hunting following several years as a soldier in the Blues and Royals. At first glance his pack appears to have been bred along modern English lines, but there is also an infusion of fell hound blood from the Ullswater, which Hume values for its independence and steadiness to riot.

Surveying the crowded hotel car park from the saddle of the enormous hunter Lyon-Smith has kindly provided is to absorb a timeless scene unblemished by any sign of protest, stewards or police, just scores of locals gathered to enjoy the camaraderie of a thoroughly old-fashioned meet. The boundaries of all four packs converge at Postbridge a couple of miles west, but on this special day the incumbent huntsman has the whole moor at his disposal. Hounds are first taken into the Spooners country to draw up the West Dart River towards the iconic Wistman's Wood, one of three high altitude oak woodlands that endure as relics from an ancient forest that covered much of Dartmoor before it was cleared by Mesolithic hunter gatherers around 5000BC. Here the stunted oaks and jumbled rocks through which they sprout are covered in a thick green film of moss, and clusters of dwarf bracken cling to skeletal branches like orchids in a rain forest.

The ancient wood is an eerie place at the best of times, even more so when the fog comes swirling in to choke the setting in grey mist that distorts timber and rock into surreal and ghostly apparitions. There is no fog today, just scudding grey clouds chasing shadows across the moor, and a clean skyline punctured by ragged tors overlooking grassy plains leeched of colour by the ravages of a long Dartmoor winter. The vista is splattered with stands of thick gorse, which has gradually been reclaiming the moor ever since the reduction of stocking rates by English Nature. "There's no view of rural England that cannot be improved by a pack of hounds, but even more so on Dartmoor," proclaims a bowler-hatted Richard Walton, moments before hounds open on the slopes of Hollowcombe.

A knowledgeable field watching hounds pick away at the line includes several past and present Masters, amongst them Guy Morlock who traded his hunting horn for a stalker's life on Jura, and former Modbury Harriers Master, Martin Daw, who carries an emergency shoeing kit on his saddle. Few have travelled as far as Martin Allison, who works during the week in Covent Garden for his family fruit and vegetable business but returns to field master for the Spooners at weekends. The breeze has got up and hounds take time to settle to a twisty line that doubles back so that those who were in front suddenly find themselves at the rear of the field. My horse may be a giant, but John makes light work of treacherous rocks, expertly slipping his hooves in and out of fissures that could trap and hold a less experienced mount. Hounds plunge across the East Dart into the Mid Devon country upstream of Postbridge, where the crossing is hideously boggy, rocky and clustered with prickly gorse, but every horse ploughs through safely to the far bank, only for the South Devon's MFH, Louise Watson, to flounder belly deep in an innocuous-looking path that several riders have already galloped along without incident.

When hounds check amongst a sea of gorse a shrill, lone voice proclaims the line and with the huntsman some way adrift – it's impossible to ride this country straight – Lyon-Smith, who is our Field Master for the day, acts quickly and decisively by cheering the others onto the cry. His intervention regains momentum at a critical juncture, for the pack are quickly up together once more and chiming away towards the beckoning green bulk of Fernworthy forest. Unless you are stogged – Dartmoor vernacular for being stuck in a bog – it's rare to leave the ground here, but we sail over a stone wall just as hounds disappear amongst trees groaning softly beneath the strong breeze. Hounds have run for an hour and twenty minutes, but the huge plantation has been the downfall of many a promising hunt and their huntsman blows hounds up when they check.

The field have been thinned out by this run, but Anthony Loveys Jervoise who carries a knife tucked into his breast pocket on the end of a watch chain, produces a fat cigar from inside his black coat and lights up. "There's nothing quite like savouring a cigar after a really good hunt," says the former MFH, who is still only halfway through his treat when we cross the Moretonhampstead road into the South Devon country. As their professional huntsman, Robert Metcalf, rides up with Hume to show him the way, hounds pick up a line within sight of the famous Warren House Inn, where it is claimed a peat fire has burnt continuously since 1845; like most of the surrounding land, the highest and loneliest hostelry in southern England is owned by the Duchy of Cornwall.

This hunt also ends up amongst forestry at Soussons where the field stand listening to hounds running beneath the trees with a strong cry that had been difficult to discern during the earlier, windswept hunt across open moorland. This is the first time we have been stationary all day, and a convenient moment for our Field Master's horse to lose a shoe, which is speedily replaced by countryman and former farrier with the Blues and

Royals, Ben Turpie. "Let's have a four o'clock hunt," grins Hume, on his way to draw Colin Irish's gorse after the hunt has fizzled out, much to the delight of the sporting farmer who pulls up in his old tractor in time to see six fine stags depart his covert. Unlike North Devon's Exmoor, where hounds still play a key role in managing the wild red deer, they have never been hunted here on Dartmoor.

The field has dwindled to a handful by the time we reach Laughter Hole, many of the red coats that left the meet six hours earlier having long disappeared, although word reaches us that several are propping up the bar back at the Two Bridges Hotel. Neil Cole, who farms the bleak prison ground at Princetown and comes from a stalwart hunting family, drives up on his quad bike with two collies for a chat and a nip of whisky, and shortly after his arrival hounds open above the East Dart River, which marks the boundary between the South Devon and Dartmoor hunts. It would have been fitting following the Two Bridges Hunt Club meet to have visited a fourth hunting country during the day's sport, but to the disappointment of the Dartmoor MFH and huntsman, Tom Lyle, it is not to be. When hounds leave Laughter Hole on a hunt across open country we expect them to streak away into the gloaming, but their huntsman has to nudge the pack forward beneath a sour east wind to keep the hunt going on a failing scent, until even this most determined of practitioners is forced to admit defeat.

Tired hounds shelter in the lee of a tall Devon bank as they wait for the hunt lorry to arrive, leaving seven-year-old Lily French, Jessica Mortimer, Tom Starling and me to hack back to Postbridge in the twilight leading half a dozen horses between us. Despite her long day in the saddle, the irrepressible and ever cheerful Lily urges her snow-white pony, Barney, forward every time we approach a gate declaring, "it's easier for me to open the gates as I'm so much closer to the ground." When we part beneath a silvery moon half an hour later I realise the young rider has already qualified for membership of the Two Bridges Hunt Club; no doubt she will be around to help celebrate this unique club's centenary in ten years' time.

The best of days across country

Great hunting runs with the Sinnington and
Quorn between 1990 and 2000.

*Whoever coined the phrase, 'the glorious uncertainty of the chase,' was spot
on, for there are few field sports where quite so much lies in the lap of the
gods. The fates really did have to combine to produce days such as those
described below. There had to be a stout fox, miles of accessible countryside, a
pack of hounds in form and a scent — always unpredictable — good enough
for them to hold the line across miles of varied terrain for hours on end.
Most huntsmen will agree that many of their best days came about when
least expected, and that the most eagerly anticipated ones sometimes failed
to deliver. The fear of missing out is why so many hunting stalwarts turn
out day after day in all weathers, hoping for the run of the season. They are
often disappointed, but just occasionally it all falls into place and when that
happens there is nothing in our world of field sports to beat it.*

IT'S A GIVEN that every contemporary huntsman wishes they had been plying their trade in an easier era decades earlier. And yet, when the time finally comes to surrender the horn there is a realisation that things were not quite so bad after all. That was certainly how I felt following fourteen consecutive years during which I thought of little else but foxes, hounds, horses, and country. Sadly, I am not sure that will be the case for the current generation of practitioners battling at the Covid coalface against a backdrop of increasingly stringent regulations and vigilante saboteurs.

I had the great good fortune to hunt my first pack of foxhounds across wild and woolly Dartmoor, a friendly and forgiving land of hospitable farmers, open country, and plentiful foxes, that up until the ban, were the essential ingredient for successful sport. When I moved north to hunt the Sinnington in the shadow of the North York Moors gamekeepers used to tell me, "You only need one good fox for a day's hunting." That's not strictly true, except on those rare occasions when it is. Just occasionally in every huntsman's career, a day will come along when almost everything falls into place, often against all odds and expectations.

January 22nd 1994 was such a day. We met that Saturday on the gravel outside a grand and beautiful country house, the owners of which have for long been closely connected with the Sinnington Hunt. Hill foxes were sometimes hard to find during the second half of January towards the end of the shooting season, but on this occasion, hounds opened in the bracken beds behind the meet within ten minutes of moving off. In country where they are scarce, there is always the fear of losing a fox soon after it has been found, but as hounds scorched northwards through the Wilderness and up the steep and thorny incline of Threadgold Bank the unthinkable became increasingly remote. There comes a stage during every memorable hunt when the watershed is crossed between a good run and a brilliant one, which for me was the moment the pack spilled out onto the dank brown heather and headed at racing pace into the heart of Bransdale Moor. The sporting artist, Robin Furness, emerged from his car at Ousegill Bridge to cheer us on our way, but he was the last human soul we saw for the next hour or more.

The going across wet moorland was horrendous, but Waggie, my game little mare standing all of 15.3 hands high found an easy, relentless rhythm once we reached the firmer ground of Rudland Rigg. A fine house stands at the head of Bransdale, which was home to Anne, Countess of Feversham, a former Master, formidable foxhunter and a source of endless support and encouragement to my young self. In her heyday the Countess rode side saddle in a red habit and was also the first lady to serve on the committee of the MFHA, so how fitting that having reached her former residence, our fox chose to turn eastwards having made a 6½-mile-point. Here amongst the heather, Gardiner '90 – a favourite hound by the celebrated sire, Cotswold Glencoyne '85 – suffered such a severe convulsion that both my whipper-in, Richard Mould, and I thought he was dead. To our astonishment he quicky recovered and by the time hounds had sunk the valley floor into Farndale was back at his usual place at the head of affairs.

The pack continued to hunt at top pace past places with alien names, for we were by now miles out of our own country. Spout House, Penny Hill, Monket Crags, Horn Ridge and Wass Gill all sped by in a glorious whirl as we strove to keep hounds in earshot, if not in sight. After we had covered seventeen gruelling miles, we finally ran into what we call a 'stopper' – the name is self-explanatory, but in this case it was the Farndale shoot wrapping up their last drive of the afternoon. Thankfully, the headkeeper was a good friend to hunting and there were no recriminations other than the overwhelming disappointment to have lost our fox after such a fine hunt. Perhaps it was his way of telling me something, but Frank Croft waited years before admitting that his beaters fished our dead pilot out of the infant River Dove after the hounds had killed him and moved on. We had other exceptional hunts in the Sinnington high side, but that was the first of them, and the one I will never forget.

Just over two years later the Sinnington mixed pack produced a memorable day in their lovely, unspoilt vale, which unlike the heavily shot high side, has always been well foxed. It's hard to imagine a great hunting run not getting underway until after 3pm, but it was about that time on February 28th 1996 when I cheered hounds into Richardson's plantation, which stands between the rivers Riccal and Rye. The small covert had become a sure find since being clear felled and replanted, and within minutes a fox came away across the old-fashioned rig and furrow grassland; I remember the silvery splashes where his hind feet clipped the glinting furrows as he galloped across the sodden sward like a steeplechaser. The lane beyond was lined with vehicles, but he went through the crowded footies like a knife through butter just as the leading hounds poured out of the covert, swung down the wind and hit the line off with a roar to make the hairs stand up on the back of your neck. If not quite a sea of grass, what lay ahead was certainly an ocean of wild, unspoilt country with no further roads for at least two miles.

The Sinnington vale is drained by a myriad of churning becks, most of which the pack swam at least once during the course of the next 3½ hours, undeterred by riot, livestock, electric fencing, and others hazards of the modern hunting field. At one stage they hit a wall of wet, freshly turned plough that in normal circumstances would grind down the best of them to a walk, but hounds just carried on chiming away as if it were stock-free grassland. I've had further points – six, seven and even eight miles – across the Sinnington low country, but no vale hunt lasted quite so long, or transported me so comprehensively to that magical place that only a huntsman knows, a place no huntsman ever wants to leave. After hounds had stuck resolutely to the line through consecutive fields of crowded sheep it felt as if they could not possibly lose their fox. But catching him was going to be another matter.

The pace had never been fast enough to put the fox under real pressure, and he maintained a seemingly unassailable five-minute, four-field lead for all but the last twenty minutes. By then it was car followers only, and when we had to abandon exhausted horses at the Lockwoods' farm near Brawby I was relieved to join their ranks and hitch a lift on the bonnet of a Land Rover, clasping a hunting horn commandeered from the farmhouse mantlepiece having lost mine somewhere along the way. As dusk settled across the vale, we could just discern the sinuous, ghostly blur of the pack racing in full cry through whisps of grey mist floating above the grassy banks of the River Seven. Even if we had not seen them in the gloaming, it would have been obvious from the renewed urgency and vigour of their cry that after seventeen meticulous miles, hounds were finally running in view.

With hunts like that, it was hard saying goodbye to the Sinnington in 1998 for a move to the Quorn. There was not sufficient space for such long runs on three of the four days we hunted each week, but the Friday country endured; a glorious and extensive swathe of rolling, well-fenced pasture liberally sprinkled with celebrated thorn coverts. The best of it lay within the confines of three large and historically important estates, whose owners extended a warm welcome to the hunt. We ran through them all on Friday

December 17th 1999 following a filthy, rain-lashed night. Despite finding well in the late Ulrica Murray Smith's small garden on the outskirts of Gaddesby, our fox had established a long lead with the help of several fields of sheep by the time we reached Streethill Farm. Ahead of us – and well out of the planned draw – lay the finest hunting country in the world, but as hounds gathered momentum on an improving scent, the fun could so easily have ended, for Lowesby were shooting that day. I have seldom felt more relieved than when a messenger galloped up with the welcome news that we were free to continue, and a hard-riding field were able to spread out and enjoy an exhilarating ride across the old turf and hedges of Lowesby estate.

Never mind moorland and bog, a long, fast hunt across the cream of high Leicestershire behind a straight-necked fox is about as close to hunting nirvana as it gets, and epitomises the close bond between man, horse, and hound. There is not much to beat landing in the same field as hounds astride a brave horse with the engine to relentlessly devour the turf and the guts to pick up the bit and attack each fence as it comes, spurred on by the clamour of hounds running hard in front. The hunt continued all the way to the summit of the wild Tilton Hills where the steep, rough banks confound many visitors' perception of Leicestershire hunting country. Having made a six-mile point the bitches swooped back downhill for a heaven-sent second helping of Lowesby before running onto the equally delectable Quenby and a check at Church Spinney. As I was watching hounds cast and contemplating my next move, I felt an unwelcome arm across my shoulder. Irritation evaporated when I realised it was the top-hatted and swallow-tailed Irishman, Aidan O'Connell. "That's the best hunt I've ever had" he beamed. "Outside of Ireland." Shortly afterwards the bitches regained the line and hunted on to an open earth near Keyham Bridge to conclude a fourteen-mile run and the best hunt I ever had in Leicestershire too.

PART TWO

GUN & RIFLE

The Twelfth on Arkleside

Arkleside Moor, August 12th 2003

Although it is now regarded as something of a cliché, there is no date in the field sportsman's calendar that has quite the same cachet as the Glorious Twelfth. This day in the delightful company of Martin Vallance, his guests and shoot personnel, did not disappoint and was also a reminder of just how many different individuals are employed during a day's driven grouse shooting. Martin has since departed to the heathery slopes in heaven, but not before he had transformed his beloved Arkleside into a productive grouse moor and left behind a legacy for others to enjoy in years to come.

THERE CANNOT BE many places to match the beauty of Coverdale in North Yorkshire on the twelfth of August. But by half-past ten, Martin Vallance's guests had hoped to be standing in a grouse butt enjoying the first drive of a new season – not waiting outside the Thwaite Arms for thick fog to lift and expose purple-shouldered hills on either side of the valley. The delay provides a perfect opportunity to discuss Arkleside Moor with its owner, who has a lived-in face, twinkling eyes and a passion for everything to do with grouse and the landscape they inhabit. Martin soon dispels my assumption that the fog conceals endless purple acres, "grouse certainly need heather, but this 2,000-acre moor was so seriously overgrazed when I bought it in 1996 that it was staring extinction in the face. The heather had retreated to a few hundred acres on the highest ground, and was clinging on by virtue of having three excellent moors as neighbours." For the new owner the solution was obvious: "I had to get rid of a lot of sheep," he says.

That may sound simple, but Martin first had to get to know the farmers, then persuade them to join the Countryside Stewardship scheme, which offers a financial incentive for removing sheep from the moor. "Their view was better the devil you know… and I was the devil they didn't know, however when the very first farmer I met told me a sheep's worst enemy is another sheep, I knew I was in with a chance," he remembers. Martin was so impressed by Charles Utley's philosophy that he translated his words into Latin and adopted them as the shoot motto, *Pessimus inimicus ovis alius ovis est*. Now all six farmers involved with Arkleside have joined the stewardship scheme, and a campaign to destroy bracken is providing sheep with replacement grassland. The results have been a spectacular revival in the grouse population, and a thirty percent increase in heather growth.

Having served as a salutary reminder that the best British field sports are completely at the mercy of the weather, the insidious fog retreats far enough uphill for Martin to gather his guests round for a pep talk. When he has finished explaining the shoot's numbering system he asks, "Have you got that, Captains of Industry?" Somebody questions if snipe are on the menu; no, definitely not. Neither is blackgame, which are regarded as a flagship species, although the chance to shoot one would be a fine thing. "We keep seeing a solitary blackcock, but I doubt he is going to produce any young on his own," says Martin, explaining that the species requires access to four different types of habitat within a relatively small area, and that he intends to plant up ghylls with woodland to help them.

Just as we approach the first line of butts, the last shards of mist peel back from the hills to reveal sweeping views, and thousands of dewy cobwebs shining in the morning light. Once settled, the guns wait in eerie silence for the first grouse of the season to appear. The sense of anticipation is palpable, and the question racing through everyone's mind is simply, "will this be a good year for grouse?" The answer seems to be a long time in coming. The faint tinkle of beaters' voices begins to drift towards us, followed by the crisp snap of a gun being closed, and the far-off cackle of a flag. Suddenly a covey bursts like shrapnel over the lower butts, and despite a fusillade of shots, continues unharmed. Within minutes birds are coming thick and fast, strong russet coveys on wings that flash white as they skim overhead. Michael Stone finds his rhythm with two birds from the same covey – one in front and one behind. Elsewhere birds are tumbling from the sky, and soon the silhouettes of approaching beaters break the near horizon. Headkeeper Karl Alderson's shrill blast signals the end of shooting in front of the line, and within minutes the drive is over.

Everyone has enjoyed some sport – none more so than Alan Wood, who is wreathed in smiles having killed seventeen birds from just twenty-three shots. Even for someone who has shot seven thousand pigeons since February, this is an impressive performance. Alan has been closely involved with his friend's moor from the start, and remembers the first time he saw the ground. "I said, where's the heather, Martin? It was white ground – miles of it" he laughs, "but the improvement in the last six years has been unbelievable." In fact so dramatic that it has resulted in the judges of the Purdey Awards for Conservation shortlisting the Arkleside entry for the final of this prestigious competition. The turnaround also means Martin has enough confidence to suggest sixty brace by lunchtime. His keeper, whose quiet demeanour is the perfect foil to his employer's cheeriness, reports an excellent show of birds, many of which either flew back, or were reluctant to take wing in what has become a muggy and humid morning.

It is a short walk to the butts for the next drive, where the vista of bent grass and peat hags resembles the flow country of Sutherland. In the distance the steep outline of Whernside towers dramatically above the surrounding landscape, and what look like strips of ripening corn are clearly visible against the darker backdrop of ground rolling away from its slopes. These lighter patches are actually bands of re-seeded heather, which Martin has been trying to establish for the past five years. "At last we have seen our efforts rewarded and an explosion of growth," he says happily. "Now we have big strong plants that should survive, and soon we hope to drive that ground. It's been a lot more difficult to establish heather in this part of Yorkshire than Derbyshire, where the seed came from."

Yet despite the lack of heather, the second drive proves as productive as the first. "Lost your virginity yet?" the host asks Glen Ogilvie, who is busy working his labrador after it is over. "Yes, with a right and left," someone answers on his behalf. More used to Suffolk pheasant and partridges, this is Glen's second day at grouse in twenty years. Another gun to have performed well is Richard Rusby, a solicitor from York who in his spare time runs two different pheasant shoots, frequently getting up at 5am to feed his birds.

Days at Arkleside are split into just four drives, broken by a sumptuous lunch served in a wooden shooting hut built by Alan Wood, an act of generosity that resulted in Alan being appointed a *Chasseur D'Honneur Arkleside*, a title bestowed on people, "who do a lot of work for free." As the expensive consultant who suggested himself as a suitable candidate was reminded, free is the operative word. Recipients wear a blue tie embossed with the shoot's logo of broken shotgun and shepherds crook – mere mortals are only permitted to wear an olive green one. The award carries just one privilege, but that is quite something: regular invitations to shoot grouse at Arkleside.

The interior of the hut is decorated with framed letters from appreciative guests. Having devoured too many slabs of delicious rare beef and other delicacies, I feel that no one is more deserving of an award than Martin's wife, Pip. Not only is she responsible for the lavish lunch, she has also been busy all morning working her dogs, Fozzy and Monty. The latter is a diminutive Jack Russell with a knack for retrieving grouse that embarrassed some of the better-bred canines present, the former an eye-catching Italian Spinone. Lunch certainly lives up to everyone's expectations, and the lewd jokes regaled by our host afterwards are very nearly as good as his wife's food.

At Arkleside guns walk to all of the drives, none of which are more than a short stroll from the shooting hut, with the exception of the one after lunch – a hike which has some of the less fit guests puffing and panting like a beaten fox. As we make our way to West Scrafton – 900 acres with 889 sheep gaits – it is difficult to believe we are anyway near civilisation, let alone within half-an-hour's drive of the A1. The view here is of nothing save rolling hills, and most of them on this higher ground a lovely shade of purple. As we walk Martin pays tribute to his keeper. "Karl is absolutely first rate, he was only part time when I bought the moor, he is mustard on vermin and kills over a hundred stoats a year."

Mention of vermin prompts a question on raptors, which results in a long silence as this conscientious moor owner searches for just the right words to describe a problem everyone involved with grouse is keen to see resolved. He reminds me that the hen harriers responsible for the ruination of Langholm as a grouse moor are back to their original low population levels – because there are no longer enough grouse, plovers and curlews to sustain them, nor gamekeepers to protect them from predators. He hopes to see bridges built with organisations that sometimes appear implacably opposed to acceptable solutions for a problem that is not going to fly away.

The sun emerges for the final drive of the day, bright shafts of light pouring out of the clouds to illuminate the head of Coverdale, and the neat stone walls dividing the small pastures on the opposite side of the valley. By now in superb form, the guns enjoy a fitting finish to what turns out to be a record-breaking day, and at well over a hundred brace, an increase of twenty-five percent on last year's previous best. Such occasions are invariably the product of much hard work, but I believe flanker Malcolm Pearson, with a sack full of grouse slung across his shoulders and a sprig of white heather in his tweed cap, spoke for everyone involved in the shoot when he told me on the walk home: "I can't speak too highly of Mr Vallance, he is a breath of fresh air. He has revolutionised this moor, and is the best thing to happen to Coverdale for a very long time."

Bagging a wild boar

Shooting wild boar in Sussex, March 2009

The Editor's instruction to go and shoot a wild boar anywhere in England was one of those dream assignments that occasionally fall into the sporting writer's lap. The enterprise was an adventure from start to finish, aided and abetted by the knowledgeable countryman, Al Ball, who was determined that we should succeed. I prefer stalking on two feet to sitting in a high seat, but there was no doubt that Al's method was the most likely one to succeed. During the 24 hours I spent in East Sussex I was struck by the rural character of both the location and the many people I met who cherish feral wild pigs for the sport and meat they provide.

SITTING IN A high tower overlooking a ride through woodland in rural East Sussex, I watch the sun's glow fade from silver birches beneath me. A sparrowhawk scythes through nearby conifers causing a flock of chaffinches to scramble wildly for cover and every time a blackbird chatters in alarm the call sets my pulse racing. Beyond the ride I can see greening fields and in the far distance a train chugging slowly along a broad valley. Somewhere geese are honking their way to Romney Marsh and homing crows headed straight for the hide bank sharply in horror when they see my face.

I have been waiting for more than an hour, contemplating the Editor's commissioning email in which he wrote, "*hate to stress this, but it HAS to work*" – meaning that failure to deliver is not an option. I am here to shoot a wild boar, a native British species that became extinct towards the end of the 13th century and except for introduced colonies, remained that way until the great storms of 1987 liberated farmed populations in Kent and Sussex. Other escapes and releases led to further colonies in the Forest of Dean, West Dorset and on the fringes of Exmoor and Dartmoor.

Although research unearthed much chatter about wild boar in the sporting press, I was unable track down a reputable local stalker. So I did what I always do when wanting to get the inside track on anything going on in the English countryside and scratched my head for a hunting friend in the locality. Di Grissell, the East Sussex and Romney Marsh's senior MFH did not disappoint. "Al Ball is your man," she said, and how right she was. Purveyor of birch to our best NH racecourses and Sussex countryman born and bred, Al accepted the challenge without hesitation. "I like a project," he told me. "Come down as soon as the shooting season ends and we will get you a boar."

Early in the afternoon we reconnoitred woodland under his management near Rye, where he had shown me a feed ride paddled soft by dozens of trotters. In a clearing close by stood a lone tree used by boar as a rubbing post and I was astonished to find a tide line of dried mud that reached well above my waist – "that's been made by one huge boar," Al reasoned, "I should say 400lbs at least." On walking deep into broadleaved woodland we found unearthed bluebell bulbs on which pigs love to feed, and wallows large enough for a hippo. Later we visited an orchard where trees had been bulldozed by boar activities and adjacent pasture churned up like a ploughed field.

Clearly this is not an animal that is going to be welcomed with open arms by the farming community, a fact that is recognised by DEFRA, which makes it clear in its 2008 wild boar action plan that responsibility for controlling feral wild boar lies with local communities and landowners. But this is not a job for any old gun or rifle, as it is an offence to shoot wild boar without having the species listed on your firearms certificate and the police will not do that for a calibre of less than .270.

Just under half of the respondents in an earlier DEFRA consultation advocated total eradication of wild boar, however that attitude appears to have softened – at least in this corner of south-eastern England, where the species appears to have acquired an almost mythical status amongst its supporters. The previous evening I had been shown a huge hide that could have come straight from the back of the tree-rubbing monster and been told that although wild boar signs are everywhere, they are rarely seen by the local hunt. I was astonished when Al's wife, Alexandra, told me that despite years of riding and hunting through the Sussex countryside, she had yet to see her first live wild boar. Like others I met during my visit, Al welcomes them on land under his management. "I don't see wild boar as vermin," he says, "they encourage regeneration in woodland, are good to eat and have a sporting value. They deserve to be carefully managed rather than simply shot on sight." Al had been baiting a feed ride for weeks, and he made it clear that obviously pregnant or suckling sows, piglets or the very young were definitely – and rightly – off the menu.

Back in the high seat dusk is thickening fast. A pair of amorous rabbits emerge from the undergrowth to play tag in the clearing beneath us, and when a lone crow alights yards away and caws loud and hoarse, I realise it is now too dark to see sheep grazing in fields beyond the edge of the wood. Then a muffled boom rolls out through the forest and the crow flaps clumsily away. Within a mile or so of where we are sitting someone may just have shot a wild boar, but I feel my chances slipping away with the fading light. I sense Al's disappointment. Although we have been sitting six inches apart for over two hours, not a word has passed between us. And then, as if by magic, a single rusty-coloured pig suddenly and silently appears on the ride in front of us, snout to the ground as he greedily guzzles up the wheat – and in the blink of an eye he is joined by a dozen others intent on snuffling up their evening meal in the gathering gloom.

Taken aback by the silent appearance of the herd, I watch them in fascination through the scope. Although they are still too far away for me to discern the post of the sights, I can see one especially cautious pig constantly lifting its head to glance up the ride towards us. Alert and rangy in appearance, there is little about him that reminds me of a domestic pig. I remember the advice Al dispensed when we sighted up the .308 rifle earlier: "Aim between the ear and the eye, and whatever happens, take one away from the main group." But night is drawing down and within minutes it will be too dark to shoot. I wait, and then I wait a little more. At last, a young boar – closer now – moves to one side and presents the chance of a safe, clean shot. I am momentarily blinded by the big rifle's flash, but when sight returns and the echo of gunshot subsides I can just discern the young black boar lying dead in the mud. "Congratulations," says Al. "He never knew what hit him."

The following morning my boar joins another of similar shape and size in the Gourmet Game Company's larder, where proprietor Neale Hopper tells me, "the whole ethos of eating local wild boar is catching on. The meat is almost red in appearance, has a distinct gamey flavour and a superb texture, quite unlike pale supermarket pork." Neale is supplied by a handful of trusted local stalkers, but like others I spoke to, he has become increasing concerned about the nefarious activities of "weekend warriors" – indiscriminate killers of wild boar. "We have a wonderful local resource," he warns, "but, to be perfectly frank, it is currently in danger of being exterminated." This sentiment is echoed by 15-times world champion clay pigeon shot, George Digweed, who has been responsibly culling wild boar in this area since the late Eighties. "There are a few individuals out there doing their best to eradicate them," he reveals, "and without more regulation they could end up doing just that. A tagging system should be introduced, and wild boar given a close season – you wouldn't shoot a hen pheasant on the nest, so why kill a sow with piglets? Its nothing more than killing the goose that lays the golden egg."

Al has organised a wild boar lunch to round off my visit and he has also recruited friends Johnny and Julia Williams to assist with an experiment that was intended to get us out of jail had the high seat failed. This is not to drive wild boar in the Continental style, but rather to move them forward ahead of a subtle beating line that is devoid of dogs, shouting or excessive noise. Before sampling the fabled meat, photographer Charles Sainsbury-Plaice and I hide behind a blind fashioned from hazel and spruce overlooking a well-trodden trail through the woodland. We listen for the drum of approaching porcine hooves, but hear only the mewing of an unseen buzzard somewhere high in the thermals. Ambushing wild boar with both feet on terra firma certainly feels to be more sporting than sitting in a high seat, and the heartbeat quickens when a flash of colour moves through the undergrowth towards us. Seconds later a large fox pads silently past, but when we hear the soft tap of approaching sticks, I know that this morning at least, victory belongs to the boar.

Half an hour later we are sitting in spring sunshine outside the Williams's house enjoying wild boar pâté and sausages. Sharing their smallholding with wild boar was the last thing the couple expected when they moved here from London to set up a catering business. "I first noticed pig damage in the garden a couple of years ago," Johnny says, "then one evening I went out with a torch and saw a herd just fifteen yards away. That is when I started believing the stories about wild boar roaming the Sussex countryside." Like many others – farmers, stalkers, foresters and game dealers among them – the caterer looks on the wild boar as a valued local resource, which he hopes will flourish in the surrounding countryside rather than suffer the fate that befell its predecessor in England some 600 years ago.

Shooting fit for a King

Driven day at Helmsley, November 2009

*The Helmsley, or Duncombe Park, shoot has for long held a special place
in my affections. I was privileged to shoot there on boys' days in the early
Eighties, for the brigadier mentioned in the article below was married to my
godmother. When I returned to the area as Master of the Sinnington Hunt
in 1990 the headkeeper, John Masterman, could not have been more helpful
or accommodating. We were never expected to stop hounds, and when they
occasionally ran in during the shooting season that was never a problem. John
was an artist at showing the style of superlative bird that lit up my Field
assignment in the autumn of 2009, but retired after many years of service in
2019. The land is still owned by the Duncombe family; the shoot is now let
out to a sporting agency but the Helmsley quality endures.*

THE NORTH YORKSHIRE town of Helmsley is transformed into a
shooting metropolis each winter, and on this damp November morning the

marketplace is crammed with four-wheel drive vehicles, hordes of unruly gundogs, and men dressed for sport in the surrounding hills. But there is only one shoot entitled to take its name from the small town – and you will not find its staff or guests in the marketplace. Instead, they are assembling out of the public gaze in the rear car park of the Black Swan hotel – affectionately referred to by locals as the Mucky Duck – in a discreet fashion, for the long-established and traditionally run Helmsley shoot has never felt the need to court publicity.

Originally, the sporting domain of the Earls of Feversham – one of the county's great landowning and hunting families – Helmsley estate was transformed into a serious shoot by sporting tenants Lord Ashcombe and Prince Radziwill in the Sixties, who put the deep and narrow dales for which the shoot is now renowned to good use. Famous names – Rocco Forte, the King of Spain, and Henry Ford amongst them – enjoyed famous sport in days when the words corporate and shooting were seldom mentioned in the same sentence. Theirs was grand sport dispensed in the old-fashioned Edwardian style, with the brigadier shoot manager placing the guns for each drive. Days did not become available to outsiders until Lord Ashcombe gave up his lease a decade ago having established the shoot's reputation as one of the finest in the land.

Since then, headkeeper, John Masterman, who this summer will collect his long service award at Belvoir Castle, has vastly increased the number of shooting days without compromise on quality. Shoot parties are escorted either by Lord Feversham's son, Jake Duncombe, or by the resident agent of over 30 years' standing, Ian Saggers, who is in charge of today's group of friends hailing from both sides of the Atlantic. Most have shot here before and there are broad smiles of recognition as guns reacquaint themselves with loaders they have not seen for twelve months. I recognise many of the locals too, including Lance Feathers, who until recently ran The Feathers hotel, Martin Nicholson, whose family ran the best butchers in town, gun repairer Ray Beadenall, and retired Helmsley barber, Peter Robinson.

As Ian leads the guns to pegs, placed in water meadows beneath the Fevershams' baroque family seat of Duncombe Park, the tips of pines ranged along the ridge ahead swim in and out of vision as autumn mists rise and fall like a silent grey tide. The moments of quiet before this first drive of the day are rare and absolute, unblemished by the shrill whistle of the pickers-up, the shouts of beaters or the invasive cackle of radios. Even the River Rye, flowing just yards away, glides noiselessly over the rock and shingle of her upper reaches. But that is all about to change. No sooner has the end gun reached his peg, than the first tall pheasant glides mysteriously out from the clouds and the shooting begins.

That cock bird soaring unscathed over a valley two fields wide is the forerunner of a prolonged flight of game flushed from an unseen cover crop beyond the horizon. Most are gliding high on set wings long before they reach the guns, who at first struggle to gauge the speed at which their targets are travelling, never mind whether they are gaining or losing altitude. But as the drive warms up they get the measure of November pheasants flying like January veterans, noticeably Dan Tutcher, who knocks down a stream of consistently high birds from his number one peg. "If that's the end of the line, I'll take it anytime," he beams after the drive is over. In fact, birds will be evenly distributed throughout the day.

The best drives in the Deer Park utilise deep chasms that cut into limestone hills overlooking the Rye valley, and the guns line such a ravine for Rico's, standing between great blocks of weathered stone and gnarled tree roots laid bare by centuries of rough weather. Early pheasants flit across the slit of open sky, but the drive belongs to Frenchmen tilting wings at the head of the pass to rocket down the ravine and invite a spray of gunfire as they flash in and out of sight through the tree tops. The lucky ones emerge unscathed to soar above water meadows to safety; the less fortunate fly within range of John Woodward and Nigel Hadden-Paton, whose accuracy obliges loaders lower down the line to keep careful watch for birds falling like stones around them. Afterwards someone suggests that the snap shots of this drive make easier targets than birds seen approaching from afar, but Woodward is having none of it, saying, "I think it has more to do with getting last night's port and brandy out of the system."

At the end of this drive, John Masterman pauses briefly to welcome back visitors from overseas – if there is any pressure in overseeing five beatkeepers, 13,500 acres and some 90 driven pheasant and partridge days a season the famously relaxed headkeeper conceals it well, always preferring to look after his beating line than trouble the guns. Last year this reticence resulted in some new guests offering the game cart attendant a present at the end of the day. "I pointed out that they'd got the wrong man," John remembers with a smile, "but one of them just turned around and told me not to try it on." Under his watch the shoot has expanded since it came back in hand to include partridges on formerly neglected ground, which provide weeks of extra sport at the start of the season. However, the shoot remains reassuringly traditional at heart – "there is no overage or underage, so we don't count shots or cartridges, nor do I carry a radio," Ian Saggers explains over a mid-morning mug of hot soup. This is clearly to the liking of his customers, who usually confirm dates for the following season before leaving. Despite the current harsh economic climate Ian reports no signs of that changing.

The excitement is palpable as the guns take up position for Sheep Pens, the celebrated Deer Park drive looked after by beatkeeper Rob Marsden. Sportsmen from all over the world cherish memories of this extraordinary drive where the pegs alternate between high platforms fashioned from the near vertical hillside and the rocky scree floor of the gorge itself. The pickers-up fall quietly into place, Marie Wilson and Sue Masterman way out of sight behind us, Colin and Jane Short from Bransdale are somewhere down near the river, whilst I join Peter Robinson and his labradors on the gully floor where the whispered conversation between us recalls memories of beaters' days and high birds from long ago.

Ears strain, but all we hear is the soft patter of raindrops on dead leaves. Then a faraway muted cocking betrays an approaching bird, which glides serenely into vision at a great height. Dan Tutcher stands up to the mark and fells the cock pheasant with a single, beautiful shot. Thereafter birds flow like homing starlings, to the delight of Haddon-Paton, who lets slip a huntsman's excited whoop each time he connects with a high one. So long and continuous is the stream of game that even an onlooker feels the discomfort of a neck craned permanently skywards to the action, which is varied, fast and without respite. However all good things must come to an end, and when the drive is finally over the damp gorge rings with superlatives, none more apt than Peter's observation, "You could feed off that for a month."

We leave the pickers-up to their work and drive back through Helmsley to follow a gin-clear ribbon of water upstream into Beckdale, where lunch is served inside a spacious cabin at the edge of a green glade. It was not always thus – "that's where the King of Spain and his friends used to have lunch in the old days," says, Ian, indicating a dilapidated shed on the other side of the clearing. Some of those sitting around the lunch table are involved with William Evans (a fact not lost on the loaders who dutifully wear caps emblazoned with the gunmaker's logo) and there is fulsome praise for the company's latest design, an elegant 28-inch barrel, side-plated, multi-choked 20-bore over-and-under. Named St James, the new gun has been doing the rounds this morning and performing so well that one member of the party confirms his order over pudding.

The light is weakening by the time guns reach their pegs for the Clump drive in lovely Beckdale, where a flock of long-tailed tits are busy amongst orange gold larches on the far side of the clearing. Suddenly a lone partridge bursts onto the scene, and as it goes down in a puff of feathers the tits zigzag away to safety as quick as tiny wings and long tails permit. Birds on this last drive test guns to the full, some crossing high and straight from valley rim to rim, others mimic the first trailblazing partridge by hugging the contours of the dale and drawing a fusillade of shots as they career down the line. In the middle of the drive an unusually heavy thud signals the demise of a guinea fowl caught in the crossfire, and the start of some good-natured banter between friends. After the horn has drawn down the veil on a superlative day Pat Cunningham is persuaded to pose with his bird for the camera. "Don't you get them in Texas?" someone asks. "Sure, but they're a lot bigger back home", answers the bemused American.

Someone hands me a brace of partridges and I remember letting slip earlier in the day how much I enjoy eating them. As I call out thanks to the headkeeper, who as usual is busy somewhere in the background, I think how perfectly his response – "at Helmsley we like to give everyone a special day" – sums up this remarkable shoot.

Ambushing woodcock in Ireland

Rough shooting at Glenmore in Co Donegal, December 2009

My former neighbour and fishing guru, Anthony Luke, was the architect of two days' sport and craic at Glenmore Lodge in Co Donegal, a property that he had advised Chris de Margary and Mick Hucknall to purchase. The Simply Red band members had met Anthony a few years earlier when he was assigned to guide them on a fishing holiday in Iceland. Their subsequent acquisition of Glenmore was principally for its salmon fishing on the River Finn and her tributaries, but with that came the sporting rights across a huge swathe of rural Ireland that is home to large numbers of snipe and woodcock during winter.

HAVING HOPED FOR a wringing-wet, green Co Donegal full of refugee snipe and woodcock, on this raw December morning I have fetched up in a cold, grey landscape still blighted by drifts of thawing snow. My host, Chris de Margary, is warming his feet in front of the fire inside Glenmore Lodge and explaining how he and Simply Red's Mick Hucknall acquired the shooting rights to some 24,000 acres of unspoilt rural Ireland – a ravishingly wild landscape of rough pasture, woodland and bog reaching into the heathery hills of the Blue Stack Mountains. "My first reaction was to question what we would do with so much ground; the second was where to start," recalls Chris, who five years later is living the dream, welcoming fishermen to Glenmore during the summer and rough shooting parties in winter.

Rough may be an apt description for the sport on offer, but according to the rock star turned country sportsman there is nothing with dog and gun to beat it. "This is no place for the stuffy or unfit," he says, grinning beneath his trademark mane of long blonde hair. "We give our guns a right good workout and enjoy watching them get stuck into the best shooting there is. I would rather shoot a single snipe or 'cock than any number of pheasants, and I think most of our guests feel the same way. They come here for a hunter-gatherer experience, not to shoot a large bag." Similar sentiments were expressed by William Hamilton Maxwell as far back as 1832 in his book, *Wild Sports of the West*, "The best 'cock shooting cannot be had without a good deal of fag. Like foxhunting, it is work for hardy spirits."

Hardy spirits ready for the off include sporting agent, Will Templer; itinerant fisherman, Anthony Luke, and Al Reynette-James, proprietor of an ice bar in Thailand. The late December slot in the calendar has become something of a pilgrimage for this small group of friends who prefer the pull of wet ground on weary legs, the chance of fleeting shots and the guarantee of craic to the holiday fireside back home. Half an hour later we are climbing over a rickety wire fence and plunging through snowdrifts to the first of many ambushes – "drive" seems too grand a description for a manoeuvre that rarely lasts longer than fifteen minutes, where the forward guns get into position by slugging around the periphery of a bog twice as fast as the approaching beaters.

The estate's young sporting manager, Sim Hay, looks on with approval as Al and Will stride forward purposefully to the headwaters of a small stream, whilst the other guns fall back in line with the beaters, who are sensibly wearing orange hats. "It makes my job a lot easier when the guests are experienced snipe and woodcock shots," Sim says, "they must have razor-sharp reactions to make the most of every chance, but only pull the trigger if the shot is absolutely safe." With the estate's most productive snipe bogs still frozen solid, the strategy is to concentrate on finding woodcock with the help of eager spaniels under the control of hospital worker, Eddie Ward, his children Shane and Amanda, and local dog man, John Bull. Depending on the lie of the land, some guns stand, and others walk, the only certainty is that no two beats will be the same.

The first woodcock is already dead by the time most of us spot it lying beak up on its back in a snow drift, shot quickly and safely by Al as it skimmed shoulder high above the gorse. To avoid low birds would be to squander half the opportunities that arise on days like this, but as in shooting grouse with pointers, the sport demands an acute awareness of everyone else's whereabouts – but without the benefit of open moorland or the pointer's warning of an imminent flush. If these guns are lucky a beater's shout may alert them to a bird in flight, although such tip-offs can be a mixed blessing as panic-stricken faces glance wildly in all but the right direction. Far better for the gun to hear for himself the soft flip of a rising woodcock.

As we cross a broken-down wall an unusually small but plump snipe flits away – silent, low and straight – only to drop back into soggy ground just beyond gunshot. "That's a jack," shouts Anthony, but this smaller species of snipe is legal game in Ireland, and the spaniels search in vain for a bird with the traits of Houdini. Jack snipe disappear altogether come March, migrating north to their sub-Artic breeding grounds, where they remain until colder weather drives them back south in the autumn. The migrant lifts without uttering the harsh grate often made by the common snipe and is considered such a delicacy at the Irish dinner table that the guns' failure to shoot one was the only disappointment of my visit.

There is forlorn hope of finding any kind of snipe on the high frozen hills of our afternoon playground. Black peat bogs lying between blocks of forestry are puckered tight by the frost's iron grip, and grass blades trailing the one flowing stream are sheathed in thick opaque tubes of ice. But we do find 'cock here, lying wherever forestry plantations such as the Wedding Cake (so named by Hucknall on a previous snowy visit) provide warmth and shelter, although with just four guns to man wood sides that stretch for hundreds of yards, Sim's ability to place them on known flight lines is the difference between success and failure.

When not looking after shooting parties, he and his spaniel spend winter days scouring the estate for the favourite haunts of woodcock, and noting which way they fly when flushed. "Its very much a work in progress," Sim explains, "and one that probably won't be complete for years." One such discovery is saved for the grand finale at dusk, when beaters push out the dilapidated gardens of a ruined house overlooking miles of desolate bog. Perhaps it is the shelter afforded from the bleak landscape by a windbreak of ragged pines, but woodcock seem to have a strange affinity with the eerie setting and half a dozen come forward, barely visible in the fading light unless silhouetted against the sky. When the beaters appear with glowing red faces a few minutes later they are carrying a couple and a half, and we are all picked-up.

Dinner is very much part of the fun, especially when freshly shot woodcock feature on the menu. Will Templer was looking forward to the delicacy so much that he could be spotted plucking birds furiously whenever there was a lull in proceedings during the day. No matter how many I dress for the table, I will never tire of admiring the woodcock's beautiful plumage, which has all the colours of a forest floor in autumn, or of searching for the single tiny pin feather hidden at the tip of each wing. Our evening is enhanced by the presence of Chris's wife, Sarah Brown, a singer, who happily talks guns, game and fish into the small hours, though the contrast between hunter-gatherers feasting on rare woodcock and the vocalist's recent tour with Simple Minds could hardly be more acute.

The following morning we travel west to Eddie Ward's stamping ground, where the weather has been kinder. His beaming smile welcomes us to low-lying watery plains of short, yellow grass, pregnant hedges and straggles of unkempt gorse that pulse beneath damp grey clouds with a woodcock vibe. The thaw, loosening scabs of ice from puddles, has come too late for all but the odd snipe, which we know will swarm to these bogs tomorrow. Yesterday's waist deep snow has been replaced by even deeper undergrowth which the guns attack with terrier-like enthusiasm, scurrying down muddy trails made by cattle and plunging into ravines choked with gorse and briar that resemble fox coverts to me, but are referred to as ditches by our friendly beaters.

"This is no country for old men," Chris jokes through gritted teeth after a thorny encounter has left him torn and bleeding. He may have spoken too soon, for seconds later the elder statesman of the party, Anthony Luke, drops a woodcock into the mess, which even our mustard-keen pack of spaniels assisted by Chris's wirehaired German pointer take several minutes to find. Later we move to the banks of Loch Melvin where waves slap restlessly against a shingle beach and woodcock lie in thickets of lichen-clad thorn, hazel and holly. Unlike snipe, which zigzag wildly and noisily when flushed, woodcock fly straight and silent, reserving their elusive jink for the first sight of danger and the forward guns use whatever cover they can to blend into the background. Time and again silhouettes of these superbly camouflaged birds flash briefly against grey skies or choppy water, many too quick and silent for even the sharpest guns.

The wind moves round to the east during the time it takes us to chase down ham sandwiches with mugs of hot tea for lunch, and we spend the short afternoon in a tamer parkland setting where the walls are solid and the hedges in good repair. I am thinking that this feels just the sort of place to find a pheasant when a cock bird comes hurtling down the wind only to be stopped by a fine shot, and minutes later a drake mallard is added to the bag. Both look incongruous when laid out beside two dozen 'cock and a handful of snipe at the end of the day. For me, Will's remark in the gloaming says it all. "Don't you just love it," he observes, "when a pheasant comes under the heading of various?"

In pursuit of a truly mixed bag

Moor edge day on the Raby estate, Co Durham,
October 2014

*There was something admirable and refreshing about this day, on assignment
for* Country Life *magazine, where fieldcraft amongst guns and beaters
played a prominent role in securing a varied bag of truly wild game. The
lack of elevenses, a hurried outdoor lunch and absolute stealth and silence
all contributed to the satisfaction and enjoyment of a day spent outwitting
remarkably canny quarry. If you know where to look, there are perhaps more
of such shooting opportunities available in 2023 than nearly twenty years
ago. There certainly appears to be no shortage of takers eager to pit their wits
against wild game and risk the uncertainty that is an integral part of the
sport. There is a view that days such as these may represent the long-term
future of game shooting.*

HALF OF LORD Barnard's expansive Upper Teesdale estate in Co Durham
consists of heather moorland managed primarily for grouse, but the

remaining 14,000 acres is marginal hill land, a bleak landscape of disparate white farmsteads, drystone walls and tumbling becks. Here, hill sheep and rabbits compete for grazing on high pastures strewn with sweeping beds of soft, green rushes that are home to a remarkable variety of game and wildlife. These wild hinterlands don't feature in the formal driven days, yet, each autumn, provide up to four days of superlative sport for a handful of fortunate guns who relish the challenge of outwitting truly wild game in stunning surroundings.

Headkeeper Lindsay Waddell's enthusiasm as he briefs guns on a murky November morning is palpable – and contagious. The group of six friends who have assembled from all corners of the British Isles for two days of wild bird sport hang on Lindsay's every word as he stresses the importance of stealth and silence on a day that will include blackgame, grouse and English partridge. Such emblematic species cannot be reared artificially, but thrive in these wild uplands thanks to the small team of dedicated gamekeepers who work year round to suppress vermin and improve habitat.

Guns are placed in absolute silence alongside a ragged drystone wall for the first ambush of the day – drive is too grand a description for a manoeuvre orchestrated by half a dozen beatkeepers and their spaniels – a silence that is only broken by grouse calling from the folds of misty surrounding hills. Our approach has been so quiet that a covey of blackgame sift undisturbed through the fields surrounding a deserted farmhouse barely 200 yards away, but they vanish as if by magic at the first rattle of a beater's flag. Moments later a hen pheasant clatters up from the sieve beds and soars unsaluted above the line, for cherished hens are always off-limits here. Although the dogs have pegged more rabbits on their short beat through the rushes than the guns have seen birds, it's smiles all round ten minutes later when a brace of her handsome long-spurred suitors are hung up in the game cart.

The shooting party are in good spirits, having been well catered for the previous evening by one of their number, amateur chef James Robson, who served crab fresh from the quayside of his Northumberland home and partridges wrapped in bacon. John Eastwood speaks for all when he explains what makes these days special. "There's no pressure up here and everything is relaxed amongst pals – to get a couple of birds each drive is good enough. I don't hit much at home in Hampshire," he confides, "and my friends have given up on me one by one." I am not so sure, for seconds later John brings down a high cock pheasant and a difficult woodcock in quick succession. The winter migrant splashes into a fast-flowing beck, watched by one of the beatkeepers, who races with his spaniel across broken ground to secure the prize before it is swept off downstream. On these days, every bird counts.

Sport has been so exhilarating that no one appears to notice that elevenses – another trapping of the formal driven day – have been dispensed with. Less standing around equates to more sport and I am sure this team of guns would not have it any other way, for they're about to be treated to a crack at the king of game birds. We follow the course of a winding beck deep into the hills, the stream shrinking as we climb ever higher to a stretch of moor that rarely features on big grouse days. Stoats are one of the most destructive predators on the estate and the discovery up here of a freshly killed rabbit with a bright red gash on the nape of its neck is a reminder that the war against these small but ruthless killers is never over. The first grouse appear high as driven pheasants, black bullets against a backdrop of scudding grey clouds, and the guns get stuck in with gusto, dropping several into dank brown heather that bears no resemblance to the rich purple bloom of August. "This," beams Henry Clark, who is no stranger to large bags on grand shoots, "really is the most ridiculous fun."

We return to lower ground for the most productive ambush of the day, during which a large covey of English partridge skim through the line, chortling merrily as they gather pace. Blackgame manage to avoid us until a lone blackcock with forked tail flared dark against the sky heads straight for James McAuley. Guns had been told to spare the sombre greyhen, but shoot her gaudy mate as two good summers have swelled the population to its highest level for fifteen years. The Irishman kills the bird cleanly in front, muttering "it had to be me" with a twinge of regret, for unlike some of the team he has shot blackgame before. As the sun breaks through rips in the cloud to light up distant hilltops and banish grey mist a flurry of cock pheasants stand on their tails and head for the sky; strong wild birds that are killed clean in the beak.

Lunch is a hurried affair, taken standing up with backs to the cool breeze as if both guns and beaters are eager to return to the fray. Afterwards the wagon transporting them draws up beside a snipe bog where Lindsay sniffs the wind like a pointer and pronounces it strong enough to persuade snipe to curl back over the line. Headkeeper at Raby since 1976, Lindsay is a ubiquitous presence throughout the day – one moment, striding out to place guns, the next sprinting off to join the end of the beat with his Pennine pointer, Monty. The Scotsman from the Angus Glens is always busy; whether pulling sinews from a woodcock's thigh, conjuring up a replacement gun or inflating a flat tyre between drives, the current National Gamekeepers' Organisation chairman has a restless energy that belies many years at the top of his profession.

A whisp of snipe comes forward; tiny birds glinting white bellies and olive backs in quick succession as they lift from the bog before spiralling skywards like stormy leaves. Guns bent double behind a drystone wall stand up suddenly to take their shots; most snipe fly on unscathed although a brace fall like stones to Russell Hanson. Light is draining from the valley bottoms as the guns are indulged with a final grouse drive, during which large packs hurtle across a deep ghyll of dark interlocking spurs running down towards the distant Cow Green Reservoir; several tumble from the sky but the bag at dusk only runs to seven different species of game. Double figures in this department would put the seal on an epic day, and everyone is eager for a duck flight, during which teal, mallard and tufted are added to the bag and the score quickly rises to a remarkable ten. "Could have been eleven," Lindsay tells me later, "but they missed the widgeon."

Longtails on the
North York Moors
End of the season on Spaunton Moor, January 2015

After many years enjoying end of season days at Spaunton there are signs that some of the guns may at last be slowing up. House guests at Aldby no longer stay up half the night rabbiting with their host, and some have even been known to feign deafness when asked to climb to the top of a steep moorland hill, which is guaranteed to gain them a nomination for the hotly contested 'wimp of the week' award. Headkeeper George Thompson is less active these days, but he still directs operations with undiminished enthusiasm and delights in revealing the size and variety of the bag in black darkness at the end of each day.

IT'S THE PENULTIMATE day of the season and the fourteen guns that have driven from all corners of England for three days of unrivalled sport are crammed inside the small shooting hut at Barmoors on the edge of the North York Moors clasping mugs of hot coffee to ward off the cold. The walls inside are covered in photographs that depict a different world to the bleak landscape waiting for us outside – images of sunny blue skies, purple hills, August grouse and men in shirtsleeves. Such days represent the culmination of a year's work for Teessider, George Thompson, who has overseen a steady increase in both grouse and native bird populations since he became headkeeper of Spaunton grouse moor back in 1998.

Today's guests are not here to shoot grouse at all, but to thin out plentiful pheasants that have sought sanctuary on this high ground from frequent shooting in valleys far below. These refugees, which have traded a guaranteed supply of wheat and the lofty branches of a winter roost for wild seeds, bilberry shoots and a warm heather bed on the ground, carry less condition than the birds they have left behind. "They look a bit like wild Norfolk pheasants by the end of January," explains George Thompson, "and they fly just as well. We need to reduce numbers above the heather line as grouse are the priority up here. I've known pheasants shift hen grouse and other moorland birds off their nests and lay their own eggs on top – that's no good at all, for those chicks will never survive."

Except for two Spaunton virgins who have bid for this day at an auction, everyone present is part of tight-knit team that make a pilgrimage to North Yorkshire at the end of January each year. Fit, determined and competitive to a man, all treasure the invitation to participate in three consecutive days of wild and varied sport on the Winn-Darley estates, and are accompanied by dogs of various pedigree that can be relied upon to hunt with the same enthusiasm as their owners. Some are the headkeeper's trusted helpers, others are close friends of the host who stay for the duration at Aldby with George Winn-Darley's long-suffering wife, Sara, although each night guests are encouraged to eat up quick and go rabbiting until the small hours.

The chilly shooting hut falls silent when the host calls for attention – everyone knows what's coming but there are still ripples of laughter when guests are reminded what they cannot shoot, and that they have been invited to perform an important job. "Everything legal and in season is on the menu," says Winn-Darley, "but we don't want any gentlemanly behaviour as far as pheasants are concerned. Anyone leaving a bird for his neighbour is going to be in trouble." Such conduct is also likely to result in the offender being nominated for the 'wimp of the week' award, which casts a long shadow over every failure in the field, no matter how small.

The day starts as it has always done with a long sweeping walk following the infant River Seven upstream towards Rosedale. No one needs to be told what to do here – the best and most confident shots plunge hurriedly down a steep, boulder-strewn hillside to take up station besides a tumbling beck, whilst others line the high heather plateau above.

As if on cue, the line begins to creep slowly forward and within seconds a cock pheasant clatters up from the heather in a shower of snow dust and is summarily dispatched. Others follow, some surviving the first 50 yards to gain speed and altitude as they curl back over the beck far below and soar on set wings for the green forestry beyond, glinting like hailstones in the cold blue sky. The host may have cautioned against gentlemanly conduct, but chance would be a fine thing for the end guns, where birds are as high as anyone has seen all season. Tree surgeon, Wocky Whitworth, James Andrews MFH, and Digs Diggins from Hidden Norfolk rise to the occasion and tumble a succession of stratospheric birds onto the far bank of the Seven.

Guns are granted no respite until reaching a tumble of rocky boulders known as Cum Reeth a mile further north, a magnet for forestry foxes and once a sure find for the recently disbanded Farndale Hunt. Some of the local names for parts of the estate are self-explanatory, but others – Venom's Nic and Plonker's Pass – have a story behind them; the latter named after an unfortunate (ex) helper who forgot to apply the handbrake on a new pick-up at the top of a steep hill. Under the shadow of these crags the spoils of an hour-long walk are transferred from bulging game bags – woe betide the guest who turns up at Spaunton without that essential piece of equipment – into a waiting pick-up, which Thompson announces he will drive round to meet the team at the end of another long march across the moor. "Need a hand George?" quips our man from Norfolk, and everyone laughs at this shallow attempt to avoid a lung-wrenching climb to the top.

We are soon plodding uphill, boots crunching through crisp snow to expose copper bracken beneath, although the snow lies thick enough in places to smooth over deep pockets into which several guns plunge waist deep. No doubt some agree when geophysicist and successful bidder, Michael Tate, announces, "you can't bloody walk in this," but no one is going to offer sympathy and risk a wimp of the week nomination. Instead the team attack the steep slope with gusto, watching their dogs as closely as a huntsman at a check – nobody intends missing in this company, but the ultimate crime is to be caught off guard and not let off your gun at all.

A vista of dark, rolling moorland waits at the summit, where the puddles are blocks of solid ice and the northern horizon an ink-black mass of gathering storm clouds spitting out the first swirling flakes of snow. There are fewer pheasants up here on the bleak moor top, but everyone is kept on their toes for this is also serious grouse country with a thriving population that is the fruition of many years' careful management. I feel a pang of sympathy for the gun who shouts "over" in error as a black bullet skims low through the line, for the otherwise easy-going headkeeper has zero tolerance with anyone whose game ID is less than perfect – but the line holds steady and all is well.

The snowstorm has taken hold with a vengeance by the time the manoeuvre is complete, obliterating bright sun with a dense white blanket that reduces visibility to yards and stings the face of anyone daring to look north. Despite this, most guns prefer the camaraderie of the freezing game cart to the inside of a pick-up, where several warm seats are available. As we trundle slowly off the moor, a disappearing tail feather betrays a wily cock pheasant slinking away with iridescent green head bent low to the ground. By the time Winn-Darley and his three rangy black labradors have leapt off the wagon the bird has gained the sanctuary of dense heather beds a good hundred yards beyond, but he is up against gundogs that hunt like terriers and a lethally accurate owner, who shows his guests how things ought to be done by knocking down the bird at long range.

It's too cold to remove frozen waterproofs for lunch inside the Blacksmith's Arms at Lastingham, but landlord Pete Trafford doesn't bat an eyelid when a motley troop of sodden countrymen crowd into his bar. They emerge half an hour later blinking in bright sunshine that has streamed in behind the midday blizzard. The soporific combination of food, a blazing fire and a pint has not blunted anyone's enthusiasm for sport, and there is no shortage of volunteers to hurry north across a mile of broken ground to fetch the heather and gale beds back from the head of Lastingham Beck. The standing guns include the host's father-in-law and senior statesmen of the party, Giles Shepherd-Cross, Frenchman-in-exile Benoit Guerin and Les Green from Winn-Darley's Aldby estate who is accompanied by his broken-coated lurcher bitch.

Guns waiting in a white valley bottom that has already seen its quota of sun for the day shiver patiently in the shade, whilst those on the sunlit ridge above gleam like ornaments beneath the dipping sun, amongst them Dave Grewer, whose spraying work has helped suppress bracken on the estate. A lone woodcock flits silently through the line and is beyond range by the time anyone has raised their gun – the cold snap has persuaded many of these migrants south in search of milder weather, for we have seen fewer than normal for the time of year. A flurry of distant shots has guns scouring the horizon, and although the birds that come forward are high, fast and testing, the elder members of the team rise to the challenge and topple several from the cold blue sky.

It's half past four when walking guns and their dogs are dropped off at the top of Hangman's Slack for the final push; a winter day of many moods is fading fast and most shoots across the country have already drawn stumps for the night. But not this one, where the final sweep into dusk is often the most exciting and productive of the day. It's a shorter, downhill walk to guns waiting above a stand of windswept pines at the bottom of the slack – the local name for a small scrubby valley – but there are scores of pheasants in between that clatter up as dark silhouettes against a fading yellow band of light in the west. This team have the perfect balance between lightning reactions and absolute safety; all have flighted wild duck in worse light than this, although by the time it's all over the road back to Barmoors is a glistening wet band in the moonlight. "A right good day," is George Thompson's summary in Alice O'Neil's warm and hospitable kitchen later, but the team of guns are already talking excitedly about prospects for the following day.

On Lancashire's hallowed ground

Flighting pinkfeet geese under a full moon,
Altcar, December 2015

*I have always associated Altcar with the Waterloo Cup, where 64
thoroughbred greyhounds competed for a trophy so prestigious that a leading
NH trainer once told me he would rather win coursing's blue riband than
the Grand National steeplechase. The last meeting was held just before
the Hunting Act became law in February 2005, during which hundreds of
hares pitted their wits and speed against pairs of coursing greyhounds. But
when I returned to those desolate fields ten years later, I could have counted
the number of hares seen on the fingers of one hand. There was something
poignant and more than a little sad about waiting for geese beneath a full
moon besides the famous Withins coursing ground devoid of spectators,
greyhounds or hares.*

THE SOUTH-WEST CORNER of Lancashire is an area uniquely rich in the sporting history of England, and until recently the setting for two of our most celebrated sporting contests. Aintree continues to host the Grand National steeplechase each April, but the 2004 Hunting Act put paid to the Waterloo Cup, the blue riband of coursing, which was held at Altcar every February just a few miles north of the famous racecourse. I have not trodden this hallowed ground for more than a decade, but the eerie emptiness comes flooding back as I follow guns to their pegs for the first drive of the Christmas shoot on the 5,000-acre Altcar estate, the Viking name of which means 'Marsh beside the River Alt.' The shoot lies within the Moss, a soggy black pancake of fertile ground carved up by yawning dykes and lying beneath sea level between a ridge of high ground to the east and the Irish Sea to the west.

At first glance the flat and featureless landscape holds little promise for driven shooting, yet Altcar has been shot successfully since the early 20th century when owned by the Sefton family. The area is also a haven for wildfowl, especially visiting pinkfeet geese that spend the winter gleaning a living from low-lying farms and marshes. "There are times you cannot sleep at night for the noise of geese," says guest gun David Nicholson, who lives in the very heart of the Moss. "I've seen flocks so large the sky changes colour when they fly overhead." The shoot is now taken by Promatic; a Wirral-based company that designs and builds state-of-the-art automatic clay pigeon traps, and run by owner Brian Jardine. "You'll be surprised how well these birds fly," he tells me as we reach his stand. "They often get the better of visitors not used to this sort of shooting."

We are facing a storm-battered block of sodden maize with cold rain spitting in our faces. However the words have scarcely left Brian's mouth before the first partridges come streaming over the line, travelling fast and high enough to put a smile on the face of anyone who connects. Pheasants follow a minute or two later – long tails streaming in the rain as they rocket skywards, bodies dark against a smear of vanishing eastern sunlight. By the time it's all over banks of dark cloud have arrived, and birds are gathered hurriedly in pelting rain. "Keep it shut," Jardine hisses when we pull up for the next drive, running a finger across his mouth. "There's a lot of game in here. Numbers one, two, and three, grab your guns and get to the end of the line as fast as you can, and remember – no shooting until the last one is on his peg." We watch them struggling silently across ground so wet that some stands this season have been abandoned altogether, but their stealth is rewarded by the beaters putting a fine show of birds over the line.

Elevenses are taken in a wooden shooting cabin where the usual cocktails and cheery banter are complemented by delicious pheasant goujons, the speciality of a local chef. The wood-burning stove inside the hut is soon bedecked like a Christmas tree with steaming caps, coats and gloves as syndicate members from the Wirral and surrounds attempt to dry sodden clothes. Fittingly, they include a couple of Sandgrounders, the name given to those born and bred at nearby Southport, where Red Rum was trained to win a record three Grand Nationals. We emerge half an hour later to find that the storm has blown through, leaving fresh winds and brighter skies in its wake.

The second half of the day is devoted to Carr Wood, a windswept tumble of silver birch and stunted oak sheltering foxy rhododendrons, rafts of copper bracken and tangles of briar, where the strategy is to walk birds beyond a bleak clearing into a separate block of woodland for a spectacular return drive. Guns trail beaters in three distinct manoeuvres, efficiently gathering pheasants that break back with the wind. Higher still, woodpigeon are blown about like specks of grey confetti; three fall in quick succession to Jardine's gun. As the team take their stands for the final drive behind iron railings that once sheltered visiting royalty there is a chance to absorb a relentlessly barren landscape, broken only by round bales rotting on bleached stubbles and flashes of glinting floodwater. Overhead, wide skies are dotted with disparate skeins of geese battling the wind, surely a good omen for my rendezvous with pinkfeet later this evening under a full moon. Headkeeper, Sam Bell, who has seen huge changes during his 35 years at Altcar, duly offers up a masterclass in how to drive game during a prolonged and exciting grand finale, after which we return to the cabin for a bounteous Christmas feast.

Several hours later I am bumping along a farm track in the dark clutching Bell's night vision binoculars; we pull up to marvel at geese swarming like insects over flooded potatoes half a mile from us, and watch wheeling flocks dropping like stones to join the feast. Bell admits prospects look good, but tempers optimism with a wariness that is the hallmark of all who hunt wild game. "You can't take anything for granted," he chuckles. "That's why it's called a wild goose chase." Jardine has arranged for Promatic demonstrator and dedicated wildfowler, Monty Barrett, to accompany me. "Pinkfeet go crazy for little potato chits left behind by the harvester, especially when they've gone mushy after a few frosts," Barrett explains. "Geese grow in confidence the longer they are left in peace, and can stay with a field like this until it's been completely eaten off. At Altcar they are rarely disturbed."

The flight has been planned to coincide with a full moon, but Monty explains that in this corner of Lancashire, cloud cover is even more important than the lunar cycle. "There's always a glow from the lights of Southport and Liverpool," he says, "but without background cloud it's much harder to spot the birds. We've got good conditions this evening, but could do with even more wind to muffle sound. Some of these geese will be 15 or 20 years old and they know what gunfire means." A swarm of honking geese lift at our approach, and Barrett selects a stretch of dyke as the ideal place from which to ambush them on their return. He fastens his labrador to a spade before putting out a dozen decoys in several inches of water, then positions double-page spreads of a tabloid newspaper on dry ground to resemble a flock of feeding geese when seen from above, securing them with lumps of wet soil.

"You never know with geese," he whispers. "They may have returned to the estuary for a wash and brush up and a bit of gritting, or they may have gone to feed elsewhere. They might not come back at all." The air is filled by the raucous calls of scarping snipe, although even the combination of a full moon and good cloud cover is not enough to reveal their tiny bodies. Suddenly, we hear geese whickering softly overhead, and I press my face into the dirt for fear of revealing our position. "Here they come," says Barrett 30 seconds later, and I sit up just in time to mount and shoot the leader, who is heading straight for me at head height with paddles out and wings stretched wide. The bird lands with a heavy thud as the others scramble frantically skywards and my hasty second barrel goes wide. Ten minutes later another chattering group is circling above us; this time Barrett speaks to them with his goose call, bringing the small skein lower in ever decreasing circles until they are close enough for us to sit up and pick targets that show clear and black against the luminous night sky.

There are so many geese floating around that periods of waiting are regularly punctuated by moments of high excitement as successive skeins come spiralling into the decoys, where the challenge is gauging when to take the shot — too soon, and out-of-range birds bank steeply away. The night is too far gone for woodcock now, but we pick up an unlucky drake mallard during a lull in proceedings, and watch a pale pair of protected shelduck circling. Two lapwings tumble earthwards and come to rest so close to our hiding place that we can pick out their crested head plumes against silvery floodwater. Such flashes of intimacy are invariably dispelled by the sound of approaching geese and the excitement that brings, although the pitch of their cry occasionally sounds so distressed that Barrett pronounces our cover has been blown.

According to him, wildfowlers of the old school went home satisfied having killed a couple of geese, but we stay out until nearly 11pm with each goose shot destined for someone's table. As Sam Bell says, "everyone wants a goose for Christmas." After he and Monty have divided the spoils it's time to head back to my Southport hotel, so close, yet so different to the moonlit Moss, which has held me in its mesmerising thrall for several hours. As Barrett had said earlier as we waited for the first geese to show: "A tide flight on the pintail or widgeon on flashes take some beating, but outwitting pinkfeet beneath a full moon is the ultimate wildfowling experience. Quite simply, there's nothing to beat it."

A country sport rich in fieldcraft

Stalking roe deer in North Yorkshire, spring and summer 2016

This article was written seven years ago, but it already feels like a lost age of innocence; a time when I used to stalk without the modern refinements that now make the job so much easier — job being the operative word, for the roe population has increased dramatically since Covid. During the crucial doe cull in early spring I now use thermal imaging binoculars to identify deer in seconds that I used to spend hours locating, and instead of lying down in wet mud to take a shot off bipods I invariably take aim from a shooting stick that is light and instantly to hand. Without these props it would be much harder to achieve the necessary cull during the short days of February and March, but the thermals stay behind once the evenings draw out and the more sporting and bucolic pursuit of bucks takes over.

GRACEFUL, SHY AND secretive, roe deer have recovered from near extinction in Southern England towards the end of the last century to such an extent that they are now a common sight across much of mainland Britain; it's a rare day's shooting or hunting that is not enlivened at some stage by their presence. However their rapid expansion from north of the Scottish border and other isolated strongholds has been achieved at the expense of woodland ecosystems and agriculture, and the necessary management of this has created a country sport perhaps richer in fieldcraft than any other.

Stalking roe deer with a high-powered rifle is a solitary diversion that takes place when most families are either getting out of bed or sitting down to dinner. It falls into two broad categories: ambushing deer by waiting for them to emerge from cover, usually from a high seat, but any vantage point where the wind is right will do; or taking the battle to them on foot. For me, the latter method is the most rewarding, drawing deeply on the stalker's knowledge of both deer and the landscape they inhabit. Roe are crepuscular grazers and browsers with a predilection for lush grass and arable crops, young leaves and berries, none of which are plentiful by the end of a long drawn out winter, meaning that roe must travel further afield to find enough food to survive the leanest months. Not only must these journeys take place when the landscape is short of protective cover, but as the evenings draw out, they must also commence in daylight.

These factors combine to make early spring a rewarding time of year to complete the doe cull, which must be achieved by the end of March after which bucks come into season to provide further sport until burgeoning crops reclaim what has been open ground since autumn. Effective management demands ongoing observation throughout the year, especially during winter when hounds and beaters through the coverts provide an accurate indication of deer numbers. By early February I expect to have a sound knowledge of how many deer are living on the North Yorkshire estate where I stalk, and exactly where to find them. Stalking in the evening means that the prospects of encountering deer are increasing by the minute, and allows a civilised start in early March; as the days lengthen that moves forward to challenge domestic harmony.

An understanding of the wind is fundamental to success and a decision on exactly where to stalk should be left as late as possible. I like to park at least half a mile downwind of where I expect deer to be feeding – no need to insult *Field* readers by stressing the importance of closing vehicle doors quietly – and mouch slowly into the beat. March can be a cold, bitter time of year, but however hard, and from whatever quarter the wind is blowing, learn to look upon it as a friend, for there is no better ally in outwitting deer. Not only does it dictate the location, direction and tack of your stalk, wind will also drive deer from certain feeding grounds and entice them onto others. When there is but a fleeting window of opportunity, knowing where not to look is a stalk half won. My most productive sessions last spring were during a week of bitter north-easterlies when I was able to dismiss huge swathes of land as worthless, for deer dislike the cold teeth of a gale just as much as we do.

With the breeze in your face, plan a route that takes in crops, pasture and scrub sheltered in the lee of woodland and hill, taking care to move as noiselessly as possible. Avoid thick fir plantations where wood pigeons love to roost – you may be able to sneak up on a deer undetected, but you will never pass close to such a wood without sending pigeons clattering noisily into the dusk. Pause to allow pheasants time to slink home, and do not unnerve a cock bird by staring straight at him from close quarters, for the arrogant chortle as he flies off can empty the land of deer. Look ahead and plan the next 50, 100, 200 yards of your route one careful step at a time, taking great care to avoid any obstacle that could compromise the crucial silence of a successful stalk. Scour the ground at your feet for slot marks that reveal which headlands deer favour, and where they like to cross ditches and streams.

The trick in early March is to pace your arrival at the most likely spot – the longer you stalk an area the more obvious these will become – with the magical but fleeting period of gloaming when deer literally come out of the woods. If you are travelling faster on two feet than you could crawl on four limbs you are moving too quickly. I can almost guarantee that whenever I hurry across hitherto unproductive ground I will bump deer that run off into the dusk barking furiously and calling time on a blank evening. Last spring I surprised an old doe this way and immediately dropped to the ground, but was unable to take a shot as she circled me from 200 yards away, barking like a farm dog. After several fruitless encounters I staged a rare ambush based on many hours' observation; she's barking at me from the freezer now.

Stop to examine hedge backs, particularly sides warmed by the setting sun, tracing their course through binoculars. Look for movement, the beacon of a snow-white rump and patches of cover that do not fit in, for deer love to hunt hedgerows for the first buds of spring, and with so little available, often browse quickly. If possible, stand behind a screen of cover when spying, ignoring obtrusive branches and focusing the binoculars on where you want to look. When passing plantations kneel down and search between ordered rows that lie beneath the canopy. I've grassed many an unsuspecting deer that way. Don't be afraid to spy further afield too; the deer 400 yards away may be your quarry today but the one half a mile distant will be there for tomorrow, next week, or whenever the wind suits.

Once you have found a shootable deer, watch it carefully to establish the pace and direction of feeding before deciding what to do next. This is where the stalker's familiarity with the landscape comes into play; knowing which gates and gaps assist a silent passage, which beck bottoms are firm enough to walk on, where dead ground exists and a plethora of other local knowledge that facilitates an undetected approach. Sometimes it pays to cut off a corner and predict where a deer will be in fifteen minutes' time – immensely satisfying when you get it right, less so when the quarry is not seen again.

Roe often appear where seconds before there were none: remember their eyesight is not as sharp as their sense of smell and hearing. Many a stalk has been saved by standing motionless whilst a deer stares with distant cupped ears; don't move until your quarry has put down its head and resumed feeding. Patience is crucial, together with an unshakeable belief that events will unfold in your favour. Last May I watched a small group of does in fading light for what seemed like an aeon. When they eventually drifted away a young buck suddenly appeared in their place and started trotting so quickly towards me that I was able to fold him up at less than 75 yards. A minute earlier I would have given very long odds against returning with a deer that evening.

By mid-April bucks will be scraping velvet from their newly grown antlers and establishing summer territories, forcing the younger and weaker ones to take up less desirable lodgings such as orchards and overgrown gardens. These deer are easily culled, but the thoughtless removal of a dominant buck can invite displaced youngsters to over-populate and damage young woodland. I put my rifle away in mid-May and wait for the summer rut, which is normally in full flow by early August. Creeping around hoping to bump into bucks when thick undergrowth and ripening crops smother the landscape is less successful than staking out plantations that are still young enough to reveal browsing deer. A well-placed high seat comes into its own during summer, although a good natural vantage point can be equally effective provided it is located downwind of the target area.

Does come into season from late July onwards and emit shrill, high-pitched squeaks, which attract any unattached buck in the vicinity. When the weather is warm and humid these encounters are often followed by energetic courtships which can leave revealing circles of flattened vegetation. It requires exceptional skill to lure a buck from dense cover by imitating a squeaking doe with a noise that is similar to the cry made by an agitated sparrow hawk. There are artificial calls that can be used to entice a buck within range, although the time frame for doing so rarely extends beyond a magical ten days in early August. I prefer to offer up my own impression of a squeaking doe as an extension of the fieldcraft referred to throughout this article but can claim only limited success. It is best to choose a sheltered clearing so that an inquisitive buck does not have to cross open ground to investigate and, as always, to remember the importance of patience. A cautious buck can take up to twenty minutes to arrive, often appearing just when the stalker is about to give up.

I have left dogs until last, but you must not leave home without one. Your canine companion should be a silent and unobtrusive shadow, pausing when you pause and ignoring the temptation to pursue other game that may appear at close quarters. A heart-shot roe can run a surprisingly long way, and most sporting breeds with half a nose soon understand what is required. Sid, our family cocker, has learnt to sit and wait whenever I start to crawl, to hold his tongue at all times and not to go after a shot deer until instructed. I would never set off to stalk without him, for it is the stalker's duty to ensure that every hit deer is accounted for.

Making a heavenly point in the Hebrides

Woodcock over pointers at Hamanavay, Isle of Lewis, December 2016

If this section of the book appears somewhat weighted in favour of woodcock that is because the bird is a personal favourite — enigmatic, mysterious, beautiful, always challenging to outwit, and delicious to eat. And despite what some 'conservation' celebrities tell us, numerous too. I saw as many, if not more, woodcock during the 2022–2023 season than ever before. The Eurasian woodcock is clearly in good health, which is somewhat ironic when considered against recent moves to shorten their season, which would surely be the prelude to an outright ban. Shooting woodcock over pointers is close to sporting nirvana, especially in the spectacular setting of the Outer Hebrides, which I visited on assignment for Country Life *magazine.*

THE OUTER HEBRIDES in early December present a very different landscape to the shimmering green hills, turquoise seas and white-powder beaches of high summer – it's as if the heavy rains of autumn have washed away all traces of greenery from the land and bleached the rock-strewn hills a dull and inhospitable yellow. Deer on the vast Hamanavay estate on the Isle of Lewis's west coast nudge ever lower during long winter nights in search of vanishing grass, and the last runs of silvery salmon and sea trout ended months ago. However, as one celebrated migrant departs, so another appears to enchant and frustrate the sportsman in equal measure. "We expect a big fall of woodcock around the time of the first full moon in November," explains the estate's stalker, Simon Hunt, "and after that they just keep coming, especially if the mainland is frozen and it's mild here."

I've joined a small group of friends to take part in one of the most challenging and exciting of all field sports, for the dedicated pursuit of woodcock in wild and mountainous country is a demanding pastime unfamiliar to all but the keenest shots. Our team leader, Patrick Steuart Fothringham, is a regular visitor to this isolated landscape where the Perthshire pheasants he has forsaken would perish within weeks. "Driven shooting is predictable and easily accessible," he asserts. "However up here one has to work hard for every bird, and you never know whether to expect feast or famine." Simon has arranged for Lancashire-born dog handler Russell Hird to assist in what appears to be the impossible task of locating woodcock amongst the bleak Hamanavay hills and glens.

Russell's brought along three Hungarian Vizlas – considered by some to be the ultimate dog for hunting upland game – and a striking red Irish setter called Pendle to point woodcock that could be lying just about anywhere on the rugged, heathery moorland known as High Bog, where the going is as treacherous as the name implies. "Walking up in a line would be fraught with difficulty as the ground is so rough; this way you can stand back and watch," Russell attests. "Once the dogs are on point it's up to the guns to use their savvy and knowledge to get into position for a safe shot as quickly as possible. There's a lot of fieldcraft involved." It's a beautiful frosty morning; quite unlike the Outer Hebrides should be at this time of year, with a cobalt-blue sky and steel-grey lochs glinting like panes of glass from the corries and glens. Russell's red Vizlas flash in and out of sight as they lope between rockfalls of ancient Lewis gneiss that are smeared with rafts of pale lichen and dimpled with green moss the texture of brushed velvet. High above us a golden eagle soars silently on sunlit wingtips, the haunting croak of an unseen raven floats out across frigid swamps and water weeps softly from every nook and cranny of the surrounding hills.

Such raw beauty is distracting, and a minute or more rushes by before any of us realise we can no longer see either of the two dogs quartering the ground ahead. However, Russell's upright stick confirms a point, and guns hurry forward with thumbs ready at the safety catch for action. The woodcock is suddenly airborne, lifting on tawny wings that fold instantly as shots ring out and the bird tumbles onto the thin ice of a frozen lochan. Ali Gemmell's young black labrador, Togo, sets off bravely to retrieve but twice tires from smashing through ice thicker than a whisky tumbler. Just when it looks as if the youngest member of our party is going to have to strip to his boxers, Togo plunges back in for one final effort and returns in triumph with the feathered brown jewel in his mouth. One 'cock in the bag, and already more drama than might be expected during an entire day potting driven pheasants.

High Bog produces several more rises, although plenty of woodcock lift so quickly that they have disappeared behind a boulder or rock face before there is a chance to shoot, only flitting back into vision when well beyond range. Others succumb to some lightning-quick shooting, combined with persistent efforts to recover every bird hit, no matter how difficult the task. Some have the single pin feather from each wing carefully removed for posterity; although sharp enough to be used as a miniaturist's paintbrush, most sportsmen are content to thread the tiny trophies through the tweed of their cap. The light easterly has been just serviceable for dogs reliant on wind to hunt, but after lunch we move to Ungeshader where pallid north-westerly slopes face out across the North Atlantic and shiver in the shade. Despite the recent full moon, woodcock are harder to find amongst these exposed hills, but there is no man born who can predict with complete accuracy exactly where such elusive game will hold. It's so quiet on this breathless afternoon that we can hear Pendle panting softly and make out the soft swish of his body brushing through heather stiffening in deference to the coming frost in this timeless landscape.

Light seeps into the corries slowly the following morning to reveal a milder grey day, with mist smouldering like damp bonfires from the slopes, and rainclouds gathering ominously out to sea. We follow the Red River upstream, finding the occasional covey of grouse, which are still in season and a welcome and exciting bonus to the bag. One cock bird is lightly pricked, but Russell's tireless workers quarter fresher and friendly wind to such good effect that it is eventually brought to book after an epic hunt. The chances are that those we miss will not see mankind again for another year, for with more than 150,000 acres of Lewis at his disposal, Russell rarely works the same ground more than once a season.

By the time we pause for lunch below the foaming waters of Loch Roanasgail, 3½ couple have been shot, and the rain has set in with a vengeance. We eat hurriedly with our backs pressed against a slab of giant rock and water trickling down our necks as we watch the bow waves of spawning salmon cutting out redds at our feet. Afterwards, Pendle's body freezes behind the upturned nose and fixed glare of a sure point, but the woodcock retreats into a narrow tunnel in the peat hags. I remove the bird gently and pass it to Russell, who smooths feathers coloured rich as autumn foliage carefully back into place before launching it to freedom. The gale snatches the bird away, and we watch until the small speck is swallowed up against a backdrop of rock and hill. "Luckiest woodcock in Scotland," someone murmurs under their breath.

Walking down the glen with the weather pressing hard at our backs is easier that marching into the teeth of a gale. Progress is much more difficult for the dogs, which must constantly turn upwind to feel for the scent. The rocks are a darker shade of grey now, and glistening like wet paint with the grassy beige plains between thrashed into perpetual frenzy by the howling wind. Woodcock are concealed in a myriad of unlikely places that offer shelter. In such wild conditions we bump several before the dogs can point them, and a brace of jinking snipe is also added to the bag before nightfall. For some of us, the long journey home took two days, yet the memories of each hard-earned and beautiful woodcock will linger for much longer than that.

Beauty, beast and a perfect view

Stalking a summer stag on the west coast of Scotland, August 2017

Of all the sporting assignments that have come my way courtesy of The Field *magazine, this was the hardest to achieve — the setbacks had nothing to do with the fieldcraft of stalking a west coast stag, but everything to do with my woeful lack of technological knowledge. Before a chance encounter with Adam and Sarah in Ullapool I was anticipating an awkward conversation with the Editor during which I would have to admit defeat simply through being unable to transfer the Swarovski scope onto my ancient rifle. Thankfully all was well once the change had been made, and the mission was accomplished during a day when everything fell miraculously into place — such is the unpredictability of hunting a wild quarry. I enjoyed using Swarovski's sophisticated binoculars for the rest of my stay on the west coast and was somewhat reluctant to post them back on my return home.*

THE COMMISSION – TO stalk and shoot a red deer stag – seemed straightforward enough; with the opportunity to test the new Swarovski telescopic sight and range-finder binoculars included, it was an assignment that I was particularly looking forward to. It was only when I attempted to fit the 30mm tube scope onto my old Mauser rifle that I realised it was not compatible with the 25mm mounts. A short drive up the west coast to visit a stalking friend yielded no joy with his rifle either, and suddenly the whole mission was in jeopardy. To further complicate matters, the friend I had invited to shoot his first stag was forced to stand down at the last minute, leaving me with no one to take out on the hill, and no rifle to fit the state-of-the-art telescopic sights languishing in the boot of my car.

Disaster was averted by a fortuitous encounter in Ullapool the following day. *Field* photographer Sarah Farnsworth and her friend, Adam Godley, were staying nearby on a work assignment, and I already knew Godley to be a competent rifle shot and experienced stalker. It was quickly established that he was travelling with his .30-06 Blaser rifle, and that he was certain its mounts would be compatible with the new Swarovski scope. A plan was hatched to take him out to shoot his first Highland stag in 48 hours' time, with Farnsworth accompanying us to take the photographs.

I began to relax a little after that, although there was another nasty scare when Godley texted me on the eve of our stalk to tell me he didn't have the hex and Torx keys necessary to remove his own scope from the rifle. I was on top of the highest hill on West Rhiconich at the time, scouring a craggy, rock-strewn landscape so rugged that the locals refer to it as the Rough Quarter. With my back to the setting sun, and overlooking the magnificent, brooding peaks of Arkle, Foinavon, and Stack, I put a call through to another helpful local. Iain answered me between hauling up lobster pots in his boat, and had delivered the tool set by the time I got home in the dark. At last, it seemed that we were all set to go.

I was away from my base on the shores of a sea loch at first light the following morning, and in a second stroke of good fortune harboured two fine stags that had eluded me the previous evening. I was able to appraise both beasts in detail through the crystal clear 8x42 lens of Swarovski's EL Range binoculars and identify the larger as a heavy, older stag that would almost certainly take to raiding local crofts this winter instead of eeking out a living on the hill. By pressing a tiny button on the binoculars, I established that he was grazing unconcernedly exactly 227 metres from where I stood; the stags were even closer than that to the march, and there was every chance they would wander into forbidden territory before settling down for the day.

There was much to do before I could revisit the stag, and an hour later I looked on as Godley fitted the new Swarovski scope in my kitchen and pronounced us ready to sight up the rifle. This was an altogether more sophisticated experience than I am used to, with the target placed at exactly 100 metres thanks to the accurate rangefinder binoculars. A shot at this comparatively close distance is most likely in rugged west coast terrain where a new horizon is breached every few minutes and each successive vista conceals as much dead ground as it presents clean. Once we appreciated the click adjustments for the Z8i scope are 1/10 mm at 100 yards the grouping was perfect, although we would have no use for some of the scope's more sophisticated features during our day in the Rough Quarter.

To my relief a good glass of the area in which I had spied the stags three hours earlier revealed the off-white tips of the older beast's antlers, protruding no more than an inch clear of the green bracken canopy in which he had lain down for the day, although there was no sign of his companion. Seen from afar, it was easy to plan what appeared to be an uncomplicated stalk into a fresh, westerly breeze. However, I warned Godley that apparently straightforward sporting challenges on the hill have a funny habit of turning into the most complicated.

We would be taking absolutely no chances, and leaving Farnsworth with a grandstand view from her comfortable seat in the heather, set off on foot for an upwind approach, gaining altitude so as to compensate for any shift in the wind, which had been of an ungenuine nature for the last few days. We had first taken stock of various landmarks including a peculiarly shaped rock, knowing that a hillside seen from afar can be very different when one starts to walk across it an hour or more later. With so much dead ground separating us from the stag lying half a mile ahead, the greatest threat to success was the risk of spooking another deer that would give our game away and put the old stag on his feet. For this reason we approached slowly but surely, taking time to scour each new vista thoroughly before moving on to the next horizon; we were not just looking for feeding or resting deer, but also scrutinizing every green bed of bracken and black peat hag for the giveaway tips of antlers. Any chance of being spotted by deer is reduced by walking in single file, for two humans side by side present twice the risk of a single silhouette; other precautions such as keeping below the skyline and avoiding sudden movements are second nature to anyone who stalks regularly on the hill.

The wind holds steady for the duration of the stalk, and there are no fresh deer to intervene. The problem presenting us, having crawled into range of the stag, is that he is showing no inclination to stir from his sunny bed and his head and body are both obscured from sight. The range finder confirms the antlers are exactly 103 metres away and seen slightly from above, his companion's clean horn is now also visible for the first time since 6.30am this morning, the twin prongs glinting like bare branches. There is no need to get any closer than this, for deer have a strange sixth sense that takes over when in close proximity of humans, however well concealed they are from smell and sight. When frightened at close range deer tend to gallop off to safety as fast as their legs can carry them, but when disturbed subtly at greater distance they often present a shootable target before wandering slowly off.

We decide to bide our time and wait for something to happen, which is often the best policy in such a situation. Thankfully the steady south-westerly keeps the dreaded midges at bay. It's time to relax for a moment and take stock of our truly spectacular surroundings: a blue loch beneath us dimpled by the rings of free-rising brownies, the surrounding hills grey-white beneath the crush of ubiquitous granite, where pockets of soil between the rocks are filled with yellowing grass, and occasional tufts of purple heather. As a backdrop to our wait, Foinavon shimmers in the heat as puffs of low white cloud dust her summit, and flashes of water glint like giant slug trails on the wet rocks of a distant cliff face. As sunlight plays across the hills a golden eagle soars into view on outstretched wings before vanishing into the wide blue void.

Despite the loveliness of our surroundings, there is only so much beauty one can absorb knowing that a shootable stag is lying well within range: the minutes pass like glue as the dilemma of a lengthy wait is considered against the risks of putting the stags on their feet. Most stalkers have their own method of making a noise that generates suspicion rather than outright alarm; some cough or bark to good effect, and during the autumn rut, a good old-fashioned roar to imitate a rival seldom fails – but on this bright, late August day hinds are the last thing on any stag's mind. It's crucial that the noise is subtle enough to prohibit headlong flight, and that the quarry is unable to work out where it came from.

None of these ploys turns out to be necessary, for the big stag suddenly and decisively gets to his feet and stares down into the blue waters of the loch beneath him. Perhaps he has heard our muted whispers, or maybe his sixth sense has kicked in, but before he has time to drift away Godley lines up the scope and squeezes the trigger. The stag drops instantly, crushing the bracken as he rolls downhill until halted by a jumble of rocks as his companion looks around trying to gauge the direction of danger. He could have been dispatched too, but we wait until the younger beast works it all out and trundles off around the shoulder of the hill.

An hour later we are enjoying a cold beer when the heavens open. The downpour lasts for an hour, and puts a seething inch of peat-brown water in every burn cascading down the hillside. It seems that our luck has even extended to the weather, and when Godley sums the stalk up as "a fabulous experience, and something I will never forget," it's time to drink a toast to our good fortune, which kicked off with that chance encounter in a small west coast town two days earlier.

PART THREE

ROD & FLY

New life on the Yorkshire Esk

Fishing for trout on the Yorkshire Esk,
summer 1983

This somewhat naive effort was my first article published by The Field, *handwritten on foolscap, and posted on spec to the magazine's Editor at the time, Derek Bingham. I was astonished when he actually printed my student endeavours, but was encouraged to continue writing about the country pursuits I so enjoyed. Much of my childhood was spent beside the beguiling Yorkshire Esk where my brother and I caught beautiful brown trout, endless salmon parr and buckets of writhing eels. Throughout that time I tried, and always failed, to catch a salmon although I do recall a small silver sea trout on a tiny dry fly. When my parents sold up and moved to the southern side of the North York Moors I forgot all about catching a salmon on the Yorkshire Esk. I finally managed to land one on the Egton beat as a guest of Olly Foster in 2021, more than forty years after my first attempt. The Esk's salmon run*

has dwindled further since the Eighties, however heavy rain during summer now brings in prolific runs of large sea trout. These days I rarely catch a brownie on my occasional visits to the river where I first learnt to cast a fly.

THE YORKSHIRE ESK, rising in the damp moorland hills, cuts its way down to the sea through the heavily-wooded and steep Esk valley in a series of swift rocky runs and dark acid pools, before discharging after its brief life into the harbour at Whitby. In years gone by the river's run of salmon and sea trout was spectacular and reports of former glorious seasons make the mouth water. In recent years the small numbers of migratory fish — which must evade not only lethal gill nets at sea but also the weaponry of poachers — landed by anglers are a sad contrast to the river's heyday.

The wild brown trout, however, are still present in good numbers and, although ignored by many, are capable of producing exhilarating sport with the dry fly. The stained acidic water suggests a food supply that is far from bountiful and, in spite of the mayfly in June, a trout which tips the scales at a pound is worthy of being called a good fish. The big fellows do exist, of course, and their lazy slurping rises can be observed at dusk, usually from under a leafy bush overhanging deep, still water.

The river had been fishing poorly in the heat of a tropical summer. When the rains arrived new life was injected into dying water and a transformation was effected within hours: the sluggish, turgid waterway became one that tumbled, angry and dirty, in its race to the sea. One of the advantages of being able to fish a river which flows within walking distance of one's home is that a prompt appearance on the bankside can be made whenever the conditions warrant it. Being in this fortunate position I was able to wander down the following evening to a river which, having cleared from the dirt of its recent spate, now flowed with the vigour of a healthy stream. The current whispered magically as it passed over rocks and boulders to tumble energetically out into brimming pools that teemed with fly life. The invigorating music of the water contrasted with the silent, deathlike progress it had made when held in the grips of a drought 48 hours earlier; where a cloak of gloom had prevailed, there was now a frenzy of activity as small brownies dimpled the stickles and glides and their older brethren cruised around the pools, periodically sucking in the feast.

Upstream at a favourite pool four or five rivulets tumble down over shallow water before blossoming out into a deep, long pool that extends for several yards beyond a sharp bend. Here a leafy hazel bush reaches its green arms and in the silent eddies, amongst flecks of foam and debris, the biggest brownies in the river cruise lazily around, safe in the shadows from any fly the angler might offer. Directly downstream the pool flows softly over the depths before the current quickens pace in a smooth glide that ruptures on shallow shingle to reform as rapids. On the far bank the entire length of the pool is overshadowed by a vertical scar of rock some fifteen feet high and smothered with a tangle of undergrowth and honeysuckle that droops, with its heavily scented apricot flowers, down to the water's edge. My attention was attracted to the head of this pool where fish were rising enthusiastically to flies coming down on the faster water. Despite liberal applications of floatant my iron blue dun found survival in such a turbulent environment too much of a struggle, and after it had drowned following several consecutive casts I changed to a larger cinnamon sedge.

I was joined on this dappled, sunlit evening by what must surely be the patron saint of hill fishermen. With a whir of black wings and a confident peep a young dipper alighted on a mossy boulder, bowed most politely three or four times as if proud of his handsome white crest, then departed upstream. Two good fish were feeding, one behind the other, in a small run which flowed into the bend. The fishing gods must have been on my side for on my first attempt the sedge alighted gently, only inches upstream of receding dimples and before it had time to drag the fish rose and took. The fight lasted only a few minutes before the explosive energy of a three-quarter-pound wild brownie suddenly died. Led meekly into the shallows, the glittering bar of gold, studded with rich, red dimples, was soon in the creel.

As I watched to select the next fish a long silver bolt hung momentarily in the air above deep waters downstream, then crashed back into the river, causing water to lap excitedly at my feet. The rains, apart from invigorating the trout population, had also brought a run of sea trout up from the estuary; I vowed to try for him when the sun finally sank. After several futile attempts trout number two was covered and hooked. Again, a brief and frenzied fight ensued before the fish was landed, this one a healthy half-pound. The light was fading fast, and the descending coolness intensified the sounds of the coming night: whirring insects, squeaking bats that flickered in the half light and the intermittent plop as fish made the most of the last of the evening flies. It felt like the time was right to try for the sea trout that had shown earlier and in the bleary dimness of dusk the sedge was exchanged for a stronger cast and a flashy Alexandra.

Fished painstakingly down stream, it produced a violent pull from a small brownie but of the sea trout there was no sign until, as I finally abandoned the waterside in darkness, an enormous splash of a large fish poured contempt on my efforts of the last hour. Nonetheless, the evening had been glorious, the fish entertaining and the weight of water looked capable of providing sport for some time to come.

Pilgrimage to marvel at Ganges mahseer

Fishing for mahseer in the upper reaches of the River Ganges, October 2004

*After spending nearly two weeks crossing the crowded Rajasthan plains it
was something of a relief to discover the wild and pristine landscape through
which the Ganges flows in her upper reaches, and to fish a river with a flow
and beauty similar to the Spey in Scotland. To have the good luck to catch
a large mahseer was the icing on the cake of a trip that was memorable for
many reasons, and not all of them good: before we set off downstream on the
final morning I wandered back up the river for a last glance at the scene of
my triumph and was shocked to find a long dead human corpse bobbing softly
in a back eddy. My companions appeared unconcerned by this discovery, but I
have often wondered what story lay behind it.*

VIKRAM AND PAVAN, two Delhi businessmen with a shared passion
for fishing, had warned me the previous evening that miles of dusty and

overcrowded plains lay between India's capital city and their secret mahseer fishing stretch on the sacred River Ganges. However, nothing could have prepared me for the tortuous journey that began before the sun rose to bake those interminable plains in a searing heat. Driving through endless towns on the way to their Shangri-La in the Himalayan foothills was a unique experience, each choking street a battlefield where water buffaloes, rickety bicycles, and a seething mass of humanity competed fearlessly for space with convoys of horn-blasting lorries, ancient cars, and motor rickshaws – not to mention the feral pigs, stray dogs, and sacred Hindu cows that miraculously thrive amongst the bedlam.

The distances between chaotic towns gradually increased until we reached the foot of a vast range of green hills, which I was told concealed the Ganges somewhere deep inside their folds. We finally arrived at a small village surrounded by terraced fields cut into the hillside, and overlooking a turquoise pool where the clearer waters of a spring-fed river mingle with the Ganges' greater flow, shimmering aquamarine under the bright, midday sun. The Ganges of the Himalayan foothills is a very different river to the broad brown slick that curls languorously though the plains further downstream, where her waters act as a magnet to thousands of bathing pilgrims. Here she cuts through steep forested gorges, and her currents foam white with anger as they crash down rocky rapids and glide with a hint of menace in long blue-green ribbons through the deepest pools. These cold waters are home to the mighty mahseer, a legendary fighting fish now banished to the least accessible stretches of their habitat by the continuing onslaught from poachers, deforestation, dam building and an expanding human population.

Unlike their relatives wallowing in the warmer waters of southern India, or those living a pampered and protected existence in rivers flowing through sacred temples, the golden flanks of the Himalayan mahseer are hard-muscled from a life spent in turbulent currents. The mahseer's aggressive nature belies its membership of the carp family, which conjures up an image of sweet corn, umbrellas and canvas seats beside a lily-covered lake. Mahseer are not tempted by boilies, but are goaded into attacking the type of treble-hooked lures used by anglers to outwit pike, bass and other predatory freshwater fish around the world, although the smaller ones living amongst rapids can provide exhilarating sport on a fly rod.

Adult mahseer spend most of their lives in the deeper pools of big rivers, running up fast-flowing tributaries to spawn when monsoon spate waters arrive in August or early September. They are famously elusive, but most anglers agree the best chance of capturing a large mahseer comes when they drop back into their home river as the spawning waters recede. However this is mid-November, and instead of targeting confluence waters full of fish recuperating from spawning we are after those that have taken up residency in the big pools downstream. A fish of more than 40lbs from this region is considered to be a trophy, and qualifies the captor for automatic entry into Vikram's exclusive 40lb club. However, 70lb monsters used to be landed regularly in the days of the raj and were even presented to local villages to feast on. Nowadays all large fish are returned to the water, although I was told a small one tastes delicious when cooked fresh over a campfire.

By the time I have washed off the dust from the long journey with a dip in the Ganges' icy waters, three inflatable dinghies have been expertly bound together and loaded by Surinder and Prahlad, our two smiling guides whose features are less Indian than Nepalese. It is late afternoon when we land at a sandy beach three miles downstream, and the sun has already dipped behind the tall mountain in front of the campsite, laying a cold blanket above the river and shrouding the gorge in an eerie, pale light that is neither night nor day.

As our guides put up the spacious dome tents that will be our home for the next 36 hours Vikram picks up a spinning rod and tests the drag on the reel until he is satisfied the setting is just right – too tight and a big mahseer will break the line, too loose and the angler will have little control over his quarry. He hands over the rod as carefully as if it were a loaded gun, and gestures across eighty yards of river to where the waters ripple beguilingly around a protruding boulder. "Cast towards that rock at 90 degrees, then pick up the slack and retrieve slowly against the current – and don't move on until you have covered every inch of the run," he advises. "If a fish takes you remember to set the hook, but whatever happens don't be heavy-handed or he will snap your line like thread."

I fish without success for half an hour, but soon after Pavan takes my place his lure is grabbed by an unseen leviathan and twenty yards of line stripped from his reel before the fish comes off. Later, dinner cooked over an open fire is eaten beneath the luminous light of a full moon, and although these are near perfect conditions for catching mahseer by night, we are all too wearied from the long journey to persevere beyond midnight. I crawl into my sleeping bag and contemplate the contrast between the crowded Rajasthan plains, which I had spent the previous ten days crossing on the back of a Marwari stallion, and the wild solitude of this pristine land. Before the whisky kicks in I am sure the last thing I hear is the faint rasp of a leopard calling from the scrub somewhere far downstream.

The next morning I am surprised to find a river that has fallen six inches – snowmelt feeding the Ganges steadies by night when the temperature drops, but the waters creep up again during daylight hours as the sun warms white slopes far upstream. As the guides brew a pot of coffee Pavan casts optimistically into the awakening river – his efforts are ignored, but several fish show as languid splashes against the far bank, where sunlight moving slowly down the mountain has not yet banished the shade. After breakfast, I wander down river to speculate amongst the faster waters, picking my way carefully between giant boulders and flicking my lure with a salmon fisherman's instinct into promising riffles and glides between rocks.

Around midday I hear excited shouts rolling down the gorge, and I hurry back upstream just in time to see Prahlad wading ashore with a monstrous fish cradled in his arms. This forty-pounder is Pavan's ticket to the club of his dreams, and it would be hard to say who was wearing the bigger grin – the successful angler, or his beaming, soaking wet guide. The fish is rapturously admired from the yellow tip of an exquisitely forked tail to the beady, intelligent eyes set in a head of polished silver, the flanks sparkling with bronze scales the size of a lamb's heart. Pavan, whose day job is something high-tech with computers in Delhi, swoons like a drunk – even our congratulatory back-slapping fails to rouse him from a state of dazed confusion. This is the effect mahseer have on grown men.

Much later, as a grey mantle of dusk chills the gorge, I head upstream to explore a small cove I had spotted earlier that afternoon. Having picked my way through a maze of tangled undergrowth, I find a foaming torrent pouring into the head of what closely resembles a classic salmon pool; the crumpled creases smoothing into a dimpled pale sheet where the riverbed drops away beneath the surface. As the lure shivers silently through this deepest part of the pool, my rod is suddenly wrenched into a violent bow, and the line is torn ferociously from the reel by a gigantic hidden strength.

Waves of helplessness wash over me as I cling tightly to my rod, hardly daring to touch the reel as the fish careers wildly around the pool, and my shouts for help are drowned by the river's greater rumble.

After ten spine-tingling minutes I sense the huge fish moving compliantly towards me, only for the illusion of victory to be shattered when it whips round uncontrollably and accelerates back into deeper water. I remember thinking, absurdly; 'this is how it must feel when the brakes fail on a speeding car.' Prahlad is suddenly besides me, sliding down a wall of sheer rock to land softly as a monkey on the beach. The grey bulk shows like a submerged boulder in the failing light. When nearly beaten the fish wallows in a sluggish roll, and the scales on its huge flank glint bronze in the last shreds of light. This is Prahlad's cue to plunge waist deep into the water, and haul up the fish like an Olympic weightlifter. "Fifty-pounder, easy fifty-pounder," he jabbers hysterically whilst staggering towards Vikram and Pavan who have arrived just in time. Their astonishment at an Englishman's outrageous good fortune in landing a 45lb fish is concealed behind broad smiles – "that's probably the biggest mahseer caught from the Ganges this year," Vikram proclaims excitedly, without a trace of envy.

By nine o'clock the following morning we are treading the high mountain path back to the village, catching tantalising glimpses through the trees of the emerald Ganges gleaming far beneath us. We are followed by a line of plodding donkeys bearing our packed belongings, the first stage of a long journey back to England, where two days later I receive an email from Vikram on a dank November evening. The message describes his plans to develop exclusive mahseer fishing camps on the Ganges and other rivers in India, and finishes with, "We drank champagne to celebrate Pavan's forty pounder last night. Your party is due next time around." That is one party I have no intention of missing.

How long can a fish
walk on water?

Sailfish on the fly in the Indian Ocean
off Kiwayu, Kenya, October 2010

*George Moorhead's quote about pirates came back to haunt us both, for on the
very day this issue of* The Field *hit the newspaper stands in September 2011,
so did the story of a kidnapping and murder at Kiwayu Safari village. The
resort closed down as a consequence and for a few years the sailfish had the
ocean all to themselves. The pirates now appear to have been vanquished, and
George has opened a smaller but equally beguiling camp on Kiwayu Island,
which is separated from the mainland by a few hundred yards of aquamarine
sea. The sailfish, together with large shoals of tuna, still thrive offshore and
continue to provide superlative sport for those prepared to undertake the long
journey to reach this Indian Ocean paradise.*

"*SULI SULI*" COMES the rumble from African throats, and then again, this
time a louder staccato scream, "*Suli Suli! Suli Suli!*" Like the huntsman's

tally ho or the beaters 'cock forward, the words are urgent, excitable and a prelude to action, but here in the Indian Ocean the cry means only one thing – the sighting of a sailfish. I scan fifty yards of water churning out behind the twin propellers of our 28ft Bertram and spot an erect black fin cutting the blue in pursuit of our skittering lure, which the crew are frantically stripping back towards the boat. The sail closes aggressively on the bait just yards from the stern, black bill thrusting like a lance through the surf as the huge fish attempts to batter his prey senseless before gulping it into his wide chute of a mouth. Had the bait been laced with hooks the steel would have been set by now, and the battle on. But for George Moorhead, passionate fly fisherman and part owner/manager of the Kiwayu Safari Village on a remote stretch of the north Kenyan coast, that would be cheating. "There's only one way to catch a sailfish," he had said as we slipped out to sea at dawn, "and that's by casting a fly with the boat in neutral."

Elusive's engine is suddenly dead, the boat bobbing in surprise, and the 8ft 14wt Sage ready in my hand as the crew yank the teaser from the sailfish's throat and the dark bulk starts to subside slowly and disappointedly into the depths. This is my cue to cast and the heavy pink streamer is spotted the instant it hits water, the fish rising immediately to attack. My cast is short, but I strip in fast and am about to lift the rod for a second shot when the ocean erupts like a volcano, and I feel the surge of a heavy weight before the line goes slack and he is gone. The heart-thumping sight of an approaching sail, the fleeting sensation of holding a monstrous fish and the hollow emptiness of a failed strike – were a hotchpotch of emotions I was to experience many times that day, for the key to catching sailfish on the fly is knowing when and how to set the hook.

Perhaps that is a little unfair to our captain, Ali Mohamed, and his crew, as having worked on the *Elusive* for the past seventeen years, Captain Ali knows where to find sailfish alright (and in October they like to cruise within half a mile of the ocean drop off). However, he would be the first to admit that relatively little is known about the fastest fish in the ocean. Most sailfish caught on rod and line are tagged and released, yet they are seldom captured for a second time, and nobody round here ever seems to land a small one. As we sped seawards Ali's crew, Athman and Mohamed Haj, had fastened slabs of tuna belly to rubber lures with needle and thread, but their real skill becomes apparent as they entice fish after fish to within casting distance of the boat. Allowing the quarry to chew rubber once too often on the way in is to risk blunting a voracious appetite, but too fast a retrieve can have just the same effect.

Ali Mohamed watches as eagerly as a frigate bird from his fly bridge, ready to knock the boat into neutral the instant his crew pluck the lure from the water. At this moment the angler steps into the spotlight – and he had better not fluff his lines, for the first cast is the best chance he will have. The trick is to drop the fly behind the fish, so that the hook finds a hold when he feels steel in his scissors and sets off on a run for freedom. With a cumbersome streamer, rolling swell and a heavy 500-grain line this is easier said than done, and the fish often ends up grabbing the fly head-on or smashing it against his powerful bill, which is a signal for the angler to recast as quickly as possible. Chances are that the thwarted killer will attack the lure with the vengeance of an injured buffalo the moment it drops back into the surf.

One thing is certain; once you have hooked a sailfish on the fly there is no going back to conventional tackle. I knew this because George had sat me down in the fighting chair and explained that I was first going to catch one with a trolled lure. "After you've got a sailfish the easy way you can relax and concentrate on doing it properly," he had reasoned. When one of the rods began bucking like a mustang I watched helplessly as Athman grabbed hold of it, set the hook and felt the weight of the fish before handing it over for me to play, which is not quite how I like things to be done. There was no denying the spectacular acrobatics that followed, but once they were over the fish went deep and its capture developed into a long, pumping slog with a short, blunt rod. As I was to discover, the same battle with fly tackle feels entirely different.

Pioneered by the Americans, saltwater fly fishing has been around for a very long time, but the sport burst into the British consciousness in the late Eighties when bonefishing was suddenly all the rage. By then our friends across the Pond had already moved on from bonefish, tarpon and permit to try their luck with fly rods against billfish in the open seas. For some, the massive blue marlin will always be the holy grail of these beautiful game fish but it is so elusive and difficult to hook that its pursuit is a specialist activity, pioneered by men such as Billy Pate who landed the first ever blue marlin on a fly off the Cuban coast as long ago as 1978 – rumour has it that he has not landed another one since. The sailfish is much more accommodating, and fly fisherman have a realistic chance of success provided they choose the right place and time of year. The Americans favour Pacific destinations such Costa Rica, Guatemala and Belize for abundant numbers and close proximity to home, but for Brits it makes more sense to hop on an overnight flight to Nairobi and then fly down to the Indian Ocean.

Sailfish turn up off the Kenyan coast during October and November and hotels from Mombasa northwards offer their clientele the chance to pursue them with a fly rod, but the greatest concentrations are found further north between Lamu and the Somali border. Yes, it is impossible to escape that six-letter word, which strikes fear into the hearts of those passing through the western Indian Ocean. But for George the pirates are a blessing in disguise, as the seas in his backyard are now teeming with fish. "Personally I would rather have Somali pirates and more fish than no pirates and foreign trawlers plundering our ocean," he says. "There are not just more fish about, they seem to be getting larger every year. Don't worry" he assures me, "the pirates are not interested in us." Pirates or no pirates, it would have taken wild horses to keep me from a return to this idyllic stretch of coastline, where elusive buffalo haunt the inland scrub and packs of African wild dogs roam sand dunes overlooking pristine beaches.

By 11am the crew have teased several fish to the boat, none of which George or I have been able to hold onto for more than a few exhilarating seconds. But at last my fly sticks in the scissors of a turning fish. For a few eerie seconds there is nothing but the hum of my reel as line is ripped into the blue, but then a silver torpedo launches from the depths some 100 yards off the stern. The line lies slack as the fish sashays across the surface of the ocean, his long, thin bill shaking against blue skies like the mast of a distressed and distant yacht. I am wondering for just how long a fish can walk on water, when he vanishes beneath the waves and immediately sets off on a second powerful run. My Tibor Pacific reel is loaded with more than a third of a mile of gel-spun backing, but when the sail re-emerges for a second long dance above the blue he seems impossibly far away and the prospect of bringing him back to the boat remote.

But the acrobatics cannot last for ever, and eventually the drag of the reel kicks in and the fight moves into the closing stages as the fish is drawn slowly but inexorably towards the boat. Record-chasing anglers use tippets down to 15lb breaking strain but I have an 80lb leader, which had earlier snapped like thread when an angry fish took on line wrapped around my rod butt. There are no mistakes this time and twenty minutes later my prize is wallowing, exhausted, beside the boat. Mohamed Haj leans over and clasps the bill with both hands as Athman slips a tag in above the pectoral fin, and then both men heave the fish into the boat.

Seen beneath the African sun, this is a beast of exquisite beauty; as the sail lifts slowly up and down we marvel at lines of darkest indigo dribbling down rich chestnut flanks on to a belly of burnished silver. The celebrated sail is not the proud black triangle I imagined, but fragile and soft as silk to the touch, and I feel a sudden pang of sympathy for a predator overcome. "100lb" announces Mohamed as he holds my prize beneath the water until it is ready to swim away. "No way," George banters, "he is just telling you what you want to hear." Fifty or 100lb, it makes no difference to me. I have caught a sailfish on the fly and I never want to sit and fight one conventionally again.

Hope experience

Fishing for sea trout (and salmon) on Loch Hope
in Sutherland, August 2011

Two days on Loch Hope in the company of knowledgeable companions were educational, fascinating and productive. Bruce Sandison is no longer with us, but his Rivers and Lochs of Scotland *is an encyclopaedia of fishing destinations throughout Scotland. I would not dream of mounting an expedition to fish anywhere remote in the Highlands without first consulting his book for advice. Don O' Driscoll is the man who first introduced me to a particularly wild and unspoilt landscape not far from Hope, where I continue to lose myself amongst the hills, lochs and rivers for weeks at a time. Loch Hope is now under different ownership, and although more than a decade has passed since my resolve to return, I have never been back.*

SANDWICHED BETWEEN LOCH Eriboll in the west and the Kyle of Tongue to the east, Loch Hope drains a wild and desolate watershed in northern Sutherland that is owned in its entirety by just four sporting estates. Fed by the Strathmore River tumbling out of Glen Golly, the narrow six-mile loch lies beneath the mighty Ben Hope and flows into the North Sea via the short but beautiful River Hope. In an era that has seen sea trout catches decline all over Scotland, Loch Hope is celebrated as a fishery that continues to buck the trend by consistently yielding more than 700 sea trout a season. In his 2005 book, *Salmon Rivers of the North Highlands and the Outer Hebrides*, Andrew Graham-Stewart points out that the quality of sea trout fishing at Loch Hope is "without equal" on the Scottish mainland. And I, lucky fellow, am here to experience this sensation first-hand, and probe the reasons for Loch Hope's consistent success.

The owner of Hope estate, Nick Boileau, has arranged for me to spend a day with Bruce Sandison, a local expert who will show me how to fish the dap and work a team of wet flies from a drifting boat, traditional techniques that Nick feels are in danger of being lost. Bruce fishes a trio of flies – Ke-he on the bob, March Brown in the middle and a Silver Butcher on the point – from an 11ft rod, pitching a short downwind cast into undisturbed waters and a making a figure of eight retrieve whilst raising the rod tip, so the bob fly is travelling just fast enough to create a subtle wake on the surface that can prove irresistible to sea trout. A knowledge of where to find fish according to wind and weather is also paramount to success; but they are slow to show on this dour and unseasonably chilly August morning and by lunchtime we have elicited just a few fruitless boils.

We put to shore for a wee dram taken in the lee of worsening weather and decide to devote the afternoon to the dap. Back in the boat Bruce hands me a 17ft telescopic rod carrying an old reel with some four yards of floss attached to the backing – the material feels silky-soft and comprises a mass of thin fibres that catch the breeze like a sail and must not be allowed to get wet. Dapping is child's play compared to working a team of wet flies, for the wind does most of the work by billowing the floss out across the loch so the fly on the end of a short leader dances beguilingly up and down on the surface as the angler works the rod tip. "With dapping there is no line in the water to frighten timid sea trout," Bruce explains, "and the fly appears to be moving completely naturally." I am watching in fascination when a silver-black head pops up and goes down hard with the ragged Black Zulu. Minutes later Bruce slips his net under my first Loch Hope finnock and I am a convert to dapping for ever.

As we fish on against a backdrop of slapping waves and the harsh croaks of great northern divers, Bruce says the success of this fishery is clearly attributable to an absence of fish farms in the locality. He worries about proposals to increase the number of farmed salmon in Loch Eriboll, which lies within the twenty miles he believes sea trout travel from the Hope estuary out to sea. "We have seen how infestations of sea lice from caged fish have wiped out the once famous runs of sea trout in Loch Maree and other west coast lochs and rivers," he says, "in my view the solution is to shut down all estuarial fish farming operations and replace them with onshore facilities away from wild fish routes." Fish farming polarises opinions with the rural employment factor and an unsympathetic Scottish government pitched against fishermen and the angling press. Riparian owners wishing to reconcile commercial fish farming interests with sporting rights sometimes appear to appreciate both sides of the debate, but often with a foot, Afghan warlord style, in both camps.

Nick Boileau suggests a number of other factors that may have contributed to the success of his fishery, including a sparsely populated catchment area that has altered little during the last hundred years. "The watershed is lightly farmed," he says, "meaning there is virtually no risk from agricultural pollution, nor are we susceptible here on the north coast to airborne pollution. As the number of rods permitted to fish at any one time has remained unaltered since 1920 there is also very low fishing pressure and the two principal estates have been managed primarily for sporting interests."

Having worked on fish farms, keen fly fisherman, Don O' Driscoll really does appreciate both sides of the debate, and he joins me 48 hours later on a morning when the breeze is soft and warm from the south-west. There are eleven boats available (two of them leased to the Altnaharra hotel and the Strathmore estate) on the loch each day, and visiting anglers are strongly advised to obtain a copy of the estate's excellent fishing map before setting off. My map indicates that in this wind north-end fish will be lying either side of the Castle Buoy, so we cut the engine 100 yards short of the marker and begin a drift into what we hope will be shoals of taking sea trout. Don is sticking to wet flies on a floating line, but the dapping rod is soon pulling silver as a succession of finnock launch themselves with reckless abandon at my ungainly Black Zulu. Some chomp it in the surface film; others leap clear of the water to nail my airborne fly, describing perfect parabolas as they plop back into the loch.

The bag limit here is two fish per boat per day, with the unusual stipulation that larger fish be retained. "Some folks say that we have got that bit back to front," Hope estate stalker, Ian MacDonald, admits, "but hopefully we will never get to the stage where you cannot keep a fish for the table." Our biggest fish weighs over 2lbs; the others appear from their size to be finnock, the local name for a sea trout on its first year back from the sea. "Finnock numbers have held up remarkably well," Ian says, "but I don't think there are quite as many large sea trout about, although this season we have landed plenty around 4lbs, several during the mayfly hatch in early July, and now we are now having a fantastic August."

After a productive morning we put ashore beside the uninhabited Arnaboll cottage and enjoy a perfect picnic lunch, unblighted by rain, midges or excessive wind. The temptation is to join my dogs sprawled out beneath the warm August sun, but the glittering expanse of Middle Bay is beckoning from the south. It takes us half an hour to reach the widest part of the loch, where the west wind dictates we work the eastern shoreline either side of Black Rock, which in 1959 produced a record 17lb sea trout. We cover parallel lines of water in a succession of drifts, during which finnock splash merrily at the dap, many within yards of the shore. A local storm is brewing up in the south end, distant sheets of grey rain laying down a chill that prompts Don to change to a slow sinking line, although his Muddler on the dropper continues to punch a bulge in the surface film.

I cut the engine for the umpteenth time that day and we embark on what looks to be the perfect drift, passing close by a rocky promontory on our shoreward voyage into a sheltered bay. "This feels fishy," says Don as we float into waters darkened by the overhang of a steep wooded bank, and the words are scarcely out of his mouth when the Muddler disappears in a violent swirl. The rod buckles dangerously as line is torn from the reel. My friend fishes light, and I don't give his leader much chance as his backing disappears rapidly into the middle of the loch during a series of long, powerful runs. But hook and line both hold, and before long Don is wading ashore to contest the closing stages of the battle from dry land. A large, lean tail breaking the surface confirms what we have both suspected from the start; this is no sea trout, but a rather exceptional salmon. And so it proves, the 14lb silver ingot later being hailed by Ian MacDonald as the largest salmon to have come out of the loch for years.

The storm has blown over during the time it has taken Don to land his prize, black clouds vanquished by shafts of evening sunlight that pick out wet rocks on the face of Ben Hope. Soon we are speeding homewards beneath the peak of Scotland's most northerly Munro, heading for a column of wood smoke unfurling from the distant Ferryman's Cottage. We don't converse above the whirr of the outboard motor, but I suspect Don is pondering the irony of landing a record salmon from the finest sea trout fishery in Scotland. I ask myself a couple of questions on the way in. Is Loch Hope as good as they say? And, the crucial test, will I come back? The answer to both is yes.

Bale Mountains' wild rainbows

Fishing for rainbow trout in Ethiopia,
November 2015

Ethiopia is a country far more diverse and beautiful than stereotypical press images reveal, and this fishing expedition was preceded by a stay in the lush surroundings of a lodge beneath the Bale Mountains National Park. The streams that drain the high plateau above the lodge converge to form rivers that pulse through rocky ravines similar in character to Highland spate streams back home, and they are full of hungry rainbow trout. Flocks of goats and sheep attended by women and children frequently came down to the river to drink or move to fresh grazing via well-trodden crossing places. Despite the presence of so many fish lurking beneath the surface, it was clear the Ethiopians had no interest in catching or eating a non-native source of protein — as evidenced by the difficulty we had in persuading the proprietor of a local café to cook our catch at the end of a wonderful evening's sport.

IT IS A long six-hour drive between Addis Ababa and the small town of Dinsho, which serves as both gateway and headquarters to the Bale Mountains National Park nearly 400km south of the Ethiopian capital; a remote high plateau of Afro-Alpine terrain drained by crystal-clear streams where the heather grows tall as trees. Most visitors come to see the endemic wildlife such as Menelik's bushbuck, the graceful Nyala antelope and the jackal-like Ethiopian wolf, which has the distinction of being the rarest canid on the planet. But for me, these animals are an unexpected bonus, for I have heard that rivers draining the high plateau are home in their middle reaches to prolific populations of wild rainbow trout.

On arrival at the sumptuous Bale Mountains Lodge I am welcomed by the owner, manager and ex-British Army officer, Guy Levene, who also happens to be a very keen fisherman. Guy explains that rainbow trout inhabiting the Danka, Shaya, Tegona and Web Rivers at an altitude of around 8,500 feet on the northern edge of the Bale Mountains are descendants of stock introduced from Kenya in the early 1960s, which can be targeted all year round with rod and line by anyone who purchases a permit (a three-day licence costs the equivalent of £6) from the National Park headquarters in Dinsho, although the rivers are often out of order during the rainy season between June and September.

By law, all anglers must be accompanied by a registered guide so the following afternoon we find our man Taha – the best guide in town according to Guy – waiting patiently on a dusty roadside wearing a fisherman's waistcoat beneath a white Kobe cap, a grey wrap-around beard and a big friendly smile. They have fished together so many times that Guy has Taha's number on speed dial on his mobile, but for the visitor there are nearly always guides hanging around the National Park headquarters at Dinsho; if not, the African drums will soon rustle one up. The benefits of employing Taha become clear the moment we head off road, for he plots the passage of our vehicle through a veritable minefield of rocky boulders by gesticulating firmly, confidently and repeatedly until at last we come to rest overlooking a plunging gorge that cuts a deep black scar though the sparse yellow landscape.

We can glimpse sections of the Web River gleaming darkly as her waters snake over black volcanic rock several hundred feet beneath us; even from this distance I can see this is what Americans would call a pocket-water stream – small, intimate and delightful to fish. My first thought on reaching the river is that we would need at least another foot of water to catch fish, for the flow connecting some of the deeper pools at the end of the dry season in March is little more than a trickle, but around every corner and wherever the current is constricted between numerous rocky outcrops there are stretches of trouty turbulence.

I am going to be working my way upstream into the dusk and hurriedly put up my rod. The 6wt is a little heavy-handed on so intimate a stream but the advantage of my Orvis Frequent Flyer is that the seven-piece rod is small enough to travel comfortably as hand luggage yet robust enough to cope with many exotic species around the world. I tie a small gold head nymph onto a 4lb leader that drops into the tail of the first long pool with an audible plop. I have not yet seen any sign of a trout and am casting with dubious confidence when the line suddenly straightens beneath the lively weight of an unseen fish. I cannot identify my quarry for the fly shakes free, but I feel a second aggressive tug at the head of the same pool and marvel at the shimmering silver bar skittering across the surface – this is, and cannot be anything but, a wild rainbow trout.

It soon becomes apparent that these Web River rainbows are devoid of fear as they attack my nymph with naive impunity – most of them wrestle free before I am able to beach them in the shallows. The bag limit is five fish per session and two larger ones of more than a pound each are landed and killed on a hunch for supper, for there is no contest between fresh trout and the spongy, fermented flatbread known as injera that accompanies most Ethiopian meals. As afternoon slips into evening the gorge floods quickly with shade and the river suddenly comes alive with fish rising freely in the weakening light. Taha had earlier selected a Klinkhamer from my fly box for the evening rise, and there is just enough time to induce a handful of slashing rises from black fins stirring the surface before the African night engulfs us to a chorus of baboons chattering excitedly from the surrounding cliffs.

We climb back out of the steep gorge through darkness thick with bats and strange sounds of the night to discover a camp fire blazing beside a small tent put up by two friends spending the weekend fishing for Web River rainbows. Quentin Robb is a farmer from Tanzania who first fished these waters as a young boy, and Paul Stewart works for an NGO in Addis Ababa, which is the administrative capital of the African Union and one of the biggest diplomatic centres in the world. The friends have caught several decent fish between them, and a brace are sizzling in the frying pan whilst their captors sip cold beer. Later, when we check into hotel rooms that have concrete floors and iron bars to deter thieves or worse, I realise that camping within sight and sound of the river is a better choice than spending a night in the nearby town of Robe. Unfortunately the whole town is temporarily without water, but someone has generously supplied my room with a bucket holding just enough to either wash in or flush the loo – but definitely not both.

Hungry and thirsty, we head out onto the mean streets of Robe where Guy quickly persuades the bemused chef of a roadside café to cook our trout for supper. The fish are brought over to our table on a bed of damp lettuce, which the local dogs gulp down like raw steak, together with perfect cold beers. We pick off the pink flesh with our fingers to a backdrop of thumping African music, flickering Christmas lights and an all-pervading aroma of wood smoke and sweat hanging like cloud above a bustling mass of humanity. Eaten with generous pinches of salt, the trout are delicious and I have seldom enjoyed a meal more. Afterwards, Levene fishes into his coat pocket for a warm bottle of red wine and speaks of the journey that has led him and his wife to the Bale Mountains. By the time it's empty the hordes have vanished and we head back through deserted streets with only stray dogs and horses for company.

We do not have to wait long to appreciate why the bustling town square emptied so suddenly and so early. At 3am the town is woken up by the blast of amplified prayers that make sleep an impossibility, and before I know it, we are breakfasting with Taha on strong black coffee, scrambled eggs and ambasha in a gaudy roadside shack as night retreats outside. Half an hour later the gorge is a thin black line beneath us in the half-light. As I pick my way down to the water's edge baboons caught unawares scamper nervously for the crags, and wattled ibis flap heavily out of the way. The air is chilly enough beside the river to demand a fleece, but green juniper bushes on the higher slopes are already shimmering beneath the heat of the equatorial sun.

We had met a few locals the previous evening, but this morning herds of goats are driven by chattering women and children down dusty passes to quench their thirst and donkeys pass us on the way to market laden with bulging sacks of grain. Fishermen are still enough of a novelty here for small crowds of children to stand and stare from a discreet distance and when my fly gets caught on top of a huge boulder a small boy scrambles up the rock face to unhook it and claim a cash reward.

If the previous afternoon had been a race to beat the onset of night, this morning there is time to appreciate the character and intimacy of a river overlooked by caves, crags and towering rocky outcrops that provide both food and shelter to the trout below. I fish tight runs that fan out into long deep pools where the cliffs close in as a barrier to further progress, forcing a retreat through baboon territory before the resumption of fishing several hundred yards upstream. These isolated stretches of water are reputed to shelter huge trout that rarely venture up or downstream, although Guy tells me that he receives regular reports of fish landed between three and four pounds.

Taha is my shadow this morning, whether watching from a high vantage point or sitting on the rocks beside me, a benign and helpful presence happy to hover in the background until his services are required, but quick as lightning with the net whenever a fish is hooked. By 10am the sun is pressing down on the water like a hot, heavy hand and the overpowering smell of Africa intensifies with the heat. The mood is suddenly languid, slow and stale as fish drop back into deeper flows and seek out shade wherever it exists. If the previous evening is anything to go by, they will return with a vengeance once the sun dips, but it is time to climb back out of the enchanted gorge and admire a 14-inch beauty caught by Guy before the drive back to Addis; a long and dusty journey, but worth every minute for a rendezvous with the wild rainbow trout of the Bale Mountains.

Fly fishing adventures in Chilean Patagonia

Fishing for trout from Rio Palena Lodge in Chile, January 2020

This trip was memorable not just for the pristine beauty of southern Patagonia, but also the extraordinary variety of fishing techniques that our brilliant guides encouraged us to experiment with. During the course of three action-packed days on the water we fished rivers, lakes and streams with dry flies, heavy streamers, artificial damsel flies and nymphs. Over dinners back at the sumptuous Rio Palena Lodge I listened to my knowledgeable companions discussing the state of fishing in the USA and learnt that the health of the west coast steelhead run gave them as much cause for concern as the plight of our Atlantic salmon back home in the UK.

WE ARE DRIVING to the River Palena on the final morning of our Patagonian fishing adventure when an elegant pampas cat emerges from dense Valdivian rainforest and slinks slowly across the dirt track in front of us – an animal so rare that it's only the second one our guide, Reinaldo, has ever seen. Like the other experienced fishing guides employed by the newly opened Rio Palena Lodge some 80 miles inland from Chaiten on the Pacific coast, much of Reinaldo's life has been spent in the great Chilean outdoors, so I take the sighting as a good omen for what lies ahead. Not that it seems possible to improve upon the fly fishing adventures our group of four have already sampled during the previous three days.

Our team is headed up by Cameron Davenport, a fisherman and hunter from Colorado and angling sales manager for Eleven Experience, who is here to assess his company's latest addition to a global portfolio of luxurious adventure lodges. Davenport has brought along acclaimed photographer, Patagoniaphile and fellow American, Bryan Gregson, and Tom Bie, who founded and edits the cult USA fishing publication, *Drake Magazine*. Consequently, the chat was peppered with unfamiliar Americanisms – beats are called sections, catches are measured in inches not pounds, trout don't take the fly, they eat it, and our normal method of fishing in the UK is so unusual on many of the large Patagonian rivers that they have a special name for that too: walk and wade.

Instead, most of the fishing is done from a raft designed to carry two anglers, expertly manoeuvred with oars by a guide to within casting distance of the bank as the boat floats merrily downstream. Having been kitted out with waders, boots and tackle back at the lodge, that was exactly how Davenport and I began our first afternoon on the churning Palena. Within a hundred yards of setting off beneath a cloudless blue sky, rainbows were attacking our streamer flies as we dropped them close to the bank and stripped them back across the current with 7wt rods and sink tip lines. I can't recall how many fish we caught that afternoon – it was well into double figures – only steep-timbered banks, sparkling aquamarine waters and giant tree trunks lying like grey skeletons on the river bed, every drowned limb in sharp focus beneath thirty clear feet of water, for these dense native hardwoods sink as if wrought from lead.

When the drift ended in fading light a vehicle was waiting to whisk us back to the sumptuous new lodge complete with helicopter gleaming in the twilight from its resting place on the lawn, but more of that later. Most Brits are happy to compromise on comfort in wild places if the sport is of a high order, but there is a certain kind of international fly fisher who demands the highest quality in both spheres. Suffice to say, the most discerning clientele would be impressed by the cuisine, accommodation and service provided by lodge staff, headed up by the delightful trio of Trini, Victoria, and Michelle, the latter an artist in the mixing of delicious pisco sours. But even paradise can have its flaws: I woke early the next morning to the unwelcome sound of banal music filtering into my bedroom (sometimes, less is more, don't you think?). Once that had been addressed, I was able to absorb the bucolic sounds of a Chilean dawn. The river's reassuring murmur, raucous quacking ducks, the chucao's haunting call from dense woodland and the occasional screech of a farmyard cockerel.

We were on the road by 7am bound for the tiny settlement of Puerto Ramirez, where the powerful Futaleufu pours into the southern end of Lake Yelcho, overlooked by majestic green-shouldered, snow-capped mountains. The 45 square-mile lake is said to be a popular fishing destination but on this breathless, high-summer morning we saw just two other boats stirring her ice-green surface. We found Arturo waiting with a motorised boat to take us out into the water; our Uruguayan guide worked as a commercial fisherman before settling in Puerto Varas to run sport fishing charters targeting king salmon that also run up the River Yelcho into the lake. "This is a dream job," he told us as the boat chugged away from the bank, "but a lot of pressure too. The standards here are higher than anywhere else I know."

Arturo need not have worried. What followed was a dreamy, surreal fly fishing experience that began with a downstream drift into the lake just as several large trout ran amok beneath the far bank, ploughing into shoals of skittering salmon smolts. By the time we had floated beyond the river mouth Davenport and I had each landed fish of more than two pounds on fry imitation streamers; his, a muscled silver bar of rainbow; mine a thick-set brownie speckled with irregular fat black spots. "Now for something different," grinned our guide as we sped off across the heart of the lake. He cut the engine a hundred yards short of a reedy fringe, where, as if on cue, a large trout leapt clean out of the water and plopped back into the lake with a dragonfly clasped between its jaws. Sink tips and streamers were replaced by floating lines and artificial damsel flies, which we cast as close to the reeds as possible.

"God save the Queen," were not words I expected to hear from my American fishing buddy, but Davenport repeated the phrase several times during the next hour as we both struck prematurely at unexpectedly subtle rises. An expletive escaped my own lips when the 4x tippet snapped like thread against the weight of a heavy fish, but we did not leave that enchanted place empty-handed. Next stop, a shaded cliff face slanting into water the colour of blue ink, which we prospected with smaller terrestrial imitations. "This will be empty twice, but on the third visit there will be a big one." Arturo shrugged. "But not today it seems. Let's try the Chilean Caribbean."

During our journey to a drop off between sandy shores and deeper water the surface of the sunlit lake was frequently stippled by swarms of fleeing smolts. "*Tuna! Tuna!*" our guide exclaimed excitedly, but without a wind, large predatory trout vanished at the boat's approach. Instead we held steady on the lip of the drop off, threw out streamers and stripped them back fast. I watched a huge trout following my fly twenty foot down, but it turned short and melted back into the depths; January and February are not conducive to catching big fish in Patagonia; the real monsters are usually landed during the cooler months at the beginning and end of the southern hemisphere fishing season. We sped upriver for a fine lunch on dry land, and afterwards drifted back downstream past black and fiery-orange coliguachos, the gentle nip of which is considerably less fierce than their appearance. Sport had been slow in the afternoon heat but that changed once we offered fish fuzzy intimations of the Patagonian horsefly.

To skim low over miles of sprawling Valdivian rainforest in a small helicopter as we did early the next morning is to appreciate just how remote and inaccessible this isolated region of Patagonia really is. The lodge's retained pilot, Christian Honorato, treated us to a breathtaking, roller-coaster ride above the second largest temperate rainforest on the planet; an undulating green carpet studded with jagged white peaks and blue lakes glittering from the hollows. We touched down beside the tumultuous Azul River, which is glacial fed and no larger than a Highland stream, and caught rainbow after free-rising rainbow on small dry flies and 3wt rods. A ten-minute flight away, we found the altogether different Tigre gurgling between streamy pools teeming with mackerel-backed, tangerine-bellied brook trout, whose flanks glowed with purple, mauve, and vermillion spots according to the angle of the light. At lunchtime our guide pointed out pink clavel de campo (country buttonhole) flowers and submerged slabs of slippery white cancahua clay, which locals use to make fireplaces.

Trout throughout Patagonia are so numerous – we must have caught more than a hundred between us on the heli-fishing trip – that it's hard to believe they are not indigenous but descendants from fish introduced from Europe and the USA from 1904 onwards. The immigrants flourished and grew so rapidly that, despite the difficulties in reaching so remote a destination, Patagonia quickly acquired a reputation for superb fly fishing that has endured to this day. I doubt the fish still average between two and three pounds as Roderick Haig-Brown so eloquently describes in his 1954 southern hemisphere classic, *Fisherman's Winter*, but gigantic trout still swim the waters he fished, and many are landed every year.

By the final day it needs only one big fish to put the seal on an epic fishing adventure. We have landed hundreds of wild brownies, rainbows and brookies, but the dog days of summer have produced few twenty-inch plus fish. The rare wild cat is forgotten by the time we put into the Palena for the last time, four fishermen in two boats destined not to see another soul on our day-long journey downstream, only lapwings, upland geese, graceful blacked-necked swans and a spiral of vultures lifting from an island shingle.

Around noon our guide manoeuvres Davenport and me towards a long streamy glide where the flow is not quite deep enough to obscure the blurred stone riverbed beneath the boat. For a moment I think my conehead JJ streamer has snagged a rock, but when the line moves diagonally across the river, I feel the weight of a fish large enough for Reinaldo to row ashore so I can disembark and do battle on dry land. Ten minutes later a dour fighter lies defeated in the net; a gleaming bar of high-shouldered piscine perfection spotted like a cheetah with a taut, savannah-tinged belly to match. No one thinks to weigh or measure such an exquisite brown trout before we watch him flick a broad tail and glide purposefully back to the safety of deep water. It has been enough just to feast our eyes on a perfect example of the magnificent wild fish that will continue to draw fly fishers from all over the world to the pristine trout rivers of Patagonia.

The allure of the magical mayfly

Fishing for wild brown trout in Ryedale,
North Yorkshire, June 2021

*There is something timeless and quintessentially English about the three
small rivers that flow through this family farm in the quietest corner of
Ryedale in North Yorkshire. I have seen good and lean mayfly seasons come
and go during the four decades I have fished there, but the beautiful insect
has never yet failed to light up a few precious days in late May and early
June. Just occasionally — perhaps once or twice in a good year — I find myself
on the water surrounded by a stupendous hatch and suicidally greedy trout.
When fishing into the warm dusk against a backdrop of relentless, splashy
rises and assailed by the heady scents and sounds of early summer, it feels like
time is standing still. On one such evening the farmer wandered down to join
me, and as we watched the sun dip beneath the distant silhouette of the North
York Moors, Billy turned to me and said of the moment, "If only we could
bottle it." If only we could.*

BLACK-HEADED GULLS wheeling and swooping above the small rivers I fish during early June are a sure sign the mayfly hatch is underway, an annual bonanza that tempts the wariest of brown trout up from their lies and opportunistic gulls down from nesting colonies high on the nearby moors. For the large, juicy insects they have come to feast on, these balmy days of early summer are the culmination of two years spent as small, prehistoric-looking nymphs rootling around on the riverbed in search of food. Having swum to the surface and shed their skins to emerge as drab duns, newly hatched mayflies join a jaunty flotilla gliding downstream to the rhythm of the river's flow. Many will disappear down the gullets of greedy trout before their wings have dried sufficiently to flutter onto dry land where they undergo a second, extraordinary transformation into exquisite, fairy-winged spinners that will never feed again; instead they dance and mate in glittering clouds all along the river bank. Afterwards the female returns to the surface film, and having laid her eggs, keels over, a spent force on splayed twitching wings. She has lived for two years as an underwater grub, but just twenty-four hours as a creature of extraordinary beauty that will die slowly whilst being carried off by the same waters that nourished her throughout life.

For the past thirty years it is my good fortune to have fished three watercourses that drain the southern slopes of the North York Moors before converging within the space of a few fields at an old-fashioned pastoral farm standing at the heart of the Sinnington Hunt vale. There have been few changes here over the last three decades. Warbling curlews still return to nest each spring, iridescent kingfishers still flash past and otters – there are definitely more otters – still surface mysteriously, often no more than a brown bulge in the rippling stream, but occasionally a full frontal of eyes, whiskers, and ruffled wet throat. And perhaps most important of all, the mayfly swarms in early summer endure as reliable and prolific as ever.

Like the wildlife their farm supports, there is a reassuring permanence about the family that owns and works the land and lives according to the rhythm of the seasons. For them and me both, there is nothing to beat mayfly time, when all nature is burgeoning, and shocking green water meadows hum contentedly with the sound of bleating lambs. Our friendship was forged on or around the hunting field; hounds frolicking in the river on summer exercise, September dawns unboxing in the ramshackle farmyard and the colour and camaraderie of a winter meet with tea and cake to look forward to at nightfall. I pay no rent for the privilege of fishing here but always remember the family at Christmas. One December, I walked the hour between our farmhouses carrying a side of smoked salmon instead of the usual joint of pork. "We don't reckon much to raw fish," was all Billy said when I asked him later if they had enjoyed it. I assumed the delicacy must have ended up inside his terrier, which is entirely appropriate for my own black-and-tan workers of the same strain have been my constant companions on the riverbank, and over the years, the death of many a fat brown rat.

The largest river arrives at the farm gushing with enthusiasm and bravado but has lost her sense of urgency and acquired the mantle of maturity by the time she departs, sluggishly through the willows, a mile downstream. Many of her runs and pools have acquired names; the origins of Corner and Junction are obvious, less so Thieves' Run and Skeleton. The former christened after mink stole a brace of trout concealed beneath some dock leaves, the latter after the remains of a long dead and buried hunter (I still have one of the old horse's teeth) gradually appeared in the face of a clay bank as a dull painting fades to reveal something more profound beneath. At the furthest point of the farm a small, reed-fringed beck whose banksides sparkle with aromatic wild stocks, rushes to join the main river over seams of pristine gravel. If these streams form the southern and western boundaries of the farm, the third cleaves it neatly in half, running straight as a die into the junction pool and concealed for much of its course by precipitous brown banks of slippery clay. To catch a fish from each of these three rivers during the course of a single day is as close to trout fishing nirvana as I am ever likely to get.

The mayfly hatch has usually started by the end of May and can last until the second week of June, but there are three distinct stages. During the initial phase wild trout with orange-tinted fins and blood-red spots on their flanks take time to gain their mayfly confidence, initially wary of such easy food after months of scraping by on March Browns and meagre pickings from the river bed. The technique is to find a vantage point overlooking the water and wait patiently for a fish to rise, or more specifically for a dun to appear drying its wings on the surface film. Watch the insect like a hawk as it is carried downstream until it disappears from sight, or vanishes in the swirl of a rising fish.

That is the cue to plan your stalk, and then creep carefully into position downstream of the target on hands and knees – wading these small streams feels wholly inappropriate – and wait patiently for a second rise before casting carefully with a 7ft 4wt rod. It is the stealthy approach that matters most for this sort of fishing, not the cast itself, which is sometimes no more than flicking out a yard or two of line. A small Grey Wulff – almost a dun, but not quite a spinner – seems to get the best results during this first stage of the mayfly season, but if it is at first declined persevere cautiously without putting the fish down, and if necessary, offer something different. There should be absolutely no rush, for the ball stays in play as long as the trout keeps eating naturals, and it's not unusual to spend an absorbing half hour in the pursuit of a single, challenging fish. Sometimes the willows and undergrowth prevent a conventional approach and it may be necessary to wriggle into position from above and allow the line to unravel downstream. For these trout there really is only one chance, for the wake induced by lifting the fly to cast again will always give the game away.

Within a few days the trout get properly tuned in, cruising around like looters to grab every mayfly going; this is the start of what they call 'Duffer's Fortnight' on the grand chalkstreams down south, although it never lasts that long up here. Turn down every invitation, put work aside, and replace the Grey Wulff with a blowsy, over-the-top imitation mayfly, for right now it's a case of the bigger the better. During this crazy window of opportunity huge and seldom seen fish emerge to feast with reckless abandon, their presence often revealed by the violent smack of a heavy rise that sends wavelets lapping against the shore. Many years ago, such a clarion call from beyond the farm boundary enticed me downstream through a stupendous jungle of cow parsley, thistle and nettles to a bankside crowded with a tight mesh of chartreuse willow wands. Yet, by squeezing between them on to smears of silty beach, I was able to flick out a fly on the end of a brutally thick cast and wrestle to the shore a succession of gigantic trout that had grown too large or clever for the goosanders and otters to catch. That year the forbidden stretch acquired a new name that has stuck: The Honeypot. But it has never been quite as good since.

Eventually full-bellied discernment sets in and even tame stockies from upstream become fussy as gourmets. It is now time to match the hatch and distinguish between subtle rises as fish scarcely break the surface to suck in dying spinners, and the rude splash as they gulp down newly emerged duns. The advantage of fishing water untroubled by other anglers is the luxury of being able to observe a specific trout over several weeks, secure in the knowledge that no one else is going to come along and remove him from under your nose. This last hurrah offers a final chance to level the score with any such fish that have become wise and wary to the artificial fly.

Provided the water level remains constant, trout will not stray far from their chosen lie, so it's a case of biding time and resisting the temptation to have another flick every time you walk past the spot. This year a particularly stubborn fish took up station on a bend of the river that encouraged a straightforward approach from downstream, and when a friend came to try on the most prolific mayfly afternoon of the year, I felt assured of success. We spent an absorbing but fruitless half hour offering him different flies, however a sharp stab of steel the previous week had tempered greed with discretion. My friend left empty-handed, and with the mayfly hatch drawing to a close the prospects of landing this very large fish were becoming increasingly unlikely.

As I walked past the spot at dusk a few days later there was a splash midstream in the stippled flow. And quickly another, then a third. Even though every other fish had hunkered down for night, the elusive trout was still hard at it. After a fortnight of failure things quickly fell into place. An easy approach, another silvery splash, and my faint fly hurrying downstream to the moment of truth. Up he came, in went the hook and away went the fish in a hard-held flurry of spume. Five minutes later I cradled a huge wild brown trout in the shallows, complete with pristine tail and a grotesquely swollen belly. He would have made a fine dish with new potatoes and salad from the garden but had provided too much entertainment for that. Instead, I watched the dappled brown lump fade back into the darkening waters. Perhaps we will meet again next year.

Mackerel, summer's glittering prize

Fishing the British shoreline for mackerel,
summer 2021

*Mackerel are one of nature's bounties that we tend to take for granted, a fish
that can be almost guaranteed to form part of the recreational sea angler's
catch during the British summer months. I still land a basket of them every
August off the north-west coast of Scotland, but where I used to fill my boots
casting from the shore with a fly rod, I must now put to sea in a boat to find
them. Mackerel appear to be much less plentiful than they were only three
years ago, an observation endorsed by the Marine Conservation Society, which
recently moved the species from green to amber. The charity has called for an
end to commercial overfishing with the exception of mackerel caught by hand
line, a low-impact method where catches are strictly controlled.*

IT'S A SAFE bet that many *Field* readers will harbour fond memories of
sunny summer days spent in pursuit of that most obliging of all saltwater

fish, the gorgeous and ubiquitous mackerel. My earliest recollections date from childhood holidays on the south Devon coast, where my brother and I would wake up at dawn and scour the blue seas overlooked by our holiday cottage in the hope of seeing *Plynlimon* anchored in the bay. Days would pass without a glimpse, until one happy morning the converted trawler owned by family friends was bobbing gently in the swell. Within the hour we would be clambering on board for a nautical adventure, the highlight of which was trolling a paravane and lure off the stern for mackerel. For young schoolboys there was nothing more exciting than holding the orange cord between finger and thumb in anticipation of a distant subaqueous thump as another fish grabbed hold of the lure and was hauled into the boat quivering like an iridescent ingot of living metal. Other times we would lower sets of primitive feathers tied to rusty brown hooks into the green depths, which frequently yielded a dozen glittering prizes from a single drop.

The zebra-like stripes of black, green, and aquamarine that decorate the back of a fresh mackerel are sensationally beautiful and appear far too exotic for anything native to our shores. In common with the glorious plumage of a winter cock pheasant, they are a sight of which I will never tire. It is small wonder that the species has lent its name to an evocative British skyscape and been the inspiration for countless artists working in every medium from paint to clay. To hold a fresh mackerel in the palm of your hand (these shoal fish rarely exceed a pound and a half in weight, although the shore-caught record is a few ounces shy of 6lb) is to feel the taut, solid, and muscular body of a member of the tuna family, celebrated for taste, speed and power. As they possess no swim bladder, mackerel are able change depth with great rapidity and must keep moving on a relentless hunt through the oceans at speeds of up to 5.5 metres per second. The summer visitors traditionally arrive off the British coastline in huge, predatory shoals from late spring onwards, not moving back to deeper waters off the Shetland and Norwegian coasts until the shorter days of autumn. Beginning with springtime in Devon and Cornwall and filtering up to the west coast of Scotland by August, the jubilant words "the mackerel are in" reverberate excitedly around coastal Britain to signal the start of one of nature's most enduring bounties.

During this summer season the mackerel's quest for food is relentless, energetic, and all-consuming, for the fish must use these months to prepare for migration back to colder, deeper waters and a winter of comparative abstinence. The species' main summer prey includes sand eels, herring, sprats, and whitebait, which make the sea's surface fizz with noisy exuberance as they seek to escape the pelagic predators beneath them. Such surface activity also acts as a magnet for opportunistic seagulls, which hammer the hapless baitfish from the skies above, and advertise the presence of mackerel shoals to observant anglers. All of this makes mackerel the easiest of all fish to catch in the ocean, for they will open their large silver-framed mouths to wolf down with impunity anything resembling a smaller fish.

When the mackerel are properly 'in', shoals can be targeted with great success by casting spinners and lures from just about every seaside pier in Britain, but a personal favourite is to hunt them down with a fly rod amongst rocky coves and inlets that characterise the west coast of Scotland. In a good year – and they are far from guaranteed these days – I have seen hundreds of tiny whitebait driven so aggressively inshore by packs of mackerel that an ebbing tide leaves behind glittering heaps of tiny, marooned fish gasping for air. Every year I return to a favourite west coast bay with my fingers tightly crossed for action; hopefully, I am greeted by the welcome clatter of a massacre in full flow tight up against the rocky shoreline, which sounds like the deluge of a summer storm battering calm seas.

The mackerel hunt these sheltered coves in relays, herding their prey into shallow water and wreaking three or four minutes of carnage before dropping swiftly back into deeper water to regroup before the next savage attack. A silver Toby lobbed out into the middle of the bay seldom fails to score, but it's much more fun to sit tight and wait for the feeding frenzy to recommence within easy casting distance of a 5wt fly rod. It doesn't matter too much what fly is on the end of your cast – anything from a silver streamer to a sunray shadow will do the trick – but it's important to get the fly out as soon as the action commences. One fast strip is all it takes for a silvery green torpedo to grab the fly and tear line from the reel with a ferocity only matched by tropical bonefish. If you are quick about your work, expect to land half a dozen before the shoal vanishes for another fifteen minutes or more.

As mackerel are not readily found so close to shore, fishing from a boat is the easiest and most productive way to catch them, either by jiggling a string of feathers up and down in the water or by using a spinning rod to cast out and retrieve lures. With both methods the secret is to find and retain contact with a shoal of hunting fish. The depth at which they are feeding may change suddenly and without warning and is dictated by a combination of the quarry species, weather and tides. Letting a line of feathers down slowly on a marked line and jigging them up and down every few feet will usually pinpoint the depth, but feast can quickly turn to famine when the fish move on and are temporarily or permanently lost. Sonar fish finders (entry level models are surprisingly affordable) are the obvious answer for the regular sea angler, but perhaps a bridge too far for a *Field* reader just out to have some fun and catch enough for the pot.

Which bring us to the culinary merits of a delicious, oily fish rich in omega-3 fatty acids, although the dense flesh is quick to go off if left in hot sunshine, as endorsed by *The Cambridge Economic History of Europe*, which noted the frequent references to "stinking mackerel" in English literature. The fish has traditionally been consumed fresh in the UK, however our Gallic neighbours preserved mackerel by pickling them in copious quantities of salt.

Many rod-caught mackerel on both sides of the Channel are now gutted and thrown – literally, for the fish cooks beautifully within its own crisp skin – straight on to a beach barbeque for a feast of sweet, succulent meat easily prised away in compact white and brown chunks from a robust backbone. No other catch is quite so easy to cook in situ, which is why mackerel hotspots along our coastline are often revealed by smoke unfurling from the beach and sand dunes.

For something a little different, it takes minutes to fashion an impromptu smoker to transform mackerel fillets into tasty, smoke-infused delicacies that can be enjoyed either hot or cold. Any flameproof container with room to accommodate a metal or tinfoil grill will suffice, beneath which is sprinkled a handful of hardwood sawdust (the by-product of a logging session with the chainsaw is idea), with the fillets placed on top. The lid of the enamel casserole dish (or whatever other container has been improvised), is replaced to create a makeshift oven, which is positioned above a fire to envelop the fish in hot smoke. Delicious with horseradish sauce and buttered brown bread, the leftovers can be taken home and mashed up with pepper, fresh lemon juice and mayonnaise to provide a flavoursome pâté that will keep for several days in the fridge.

Chances are that you will catch many more mackerel than can be consumed at one sitting. If so, they can be gutted, washed off in the sea, and popped straight into the deep freeze when you get home. Forget about individual bags: just leave each fish to set solid before transferring them into a heavy-duty dustbin liner to dip into for barbeque fodder throughout summer. Try keeping some fresh ones back to create a sensational ceviche of raw mackerel cubes sprinkled with olive oil and soaked in lime and lemon juice with peppercorns and onion slices to spice up the mix. Served with pickled cucumbers and horseradish mousse, there are few fresher, better or more original starters with which to wow your guests.

Throughout our lives mackerel have been readily available for these tantalising feasts, but the signs are out there that, in common with many oceanic species, the health and habits of the species may be changing. North-east Atlantic mackerel appear to be arriving in our waters earlier and leaving later each year, which has been attributed to sea temperatures warming at up to 0.9 degrees per decade. The zooplankton that many of the mackerel's prey species rely on for sustenance thrive best in cold water, and as those organisms move ever further north, so do the herring, sprats and whitebait. Having been absent for centuries, mackerel now frequent Icelandic waters in large numbers during winter.

But all is not lost: there is no record of how many mackerel are caught each season by thousands of sport anglers and holiday makers, but we do know that 150,000 tonnes were landed by UK vessels alone from our waters during 2019. As usual with nature there is no straightforward answer and no guarantees for the future. But one thing is certain: this year, I will be after the summer visitors as soon as they arrive here in the north-east. And whether I catch them from the shore with a fly rod or with lures or feathers from a boat or Whitby Pier, I will cherish every one. For there may come a day when we can no longer take mackerel for granted.

Part Four

Mixed Bag

War of the worms

Worming grouse by night on the
North York Moors, February 2004

*I retain fond memories of my nocturnal grouse catching expedition with
George and Jill Thompson, which had much in common with numerous happy
nights spent lamping rabbits. Scientific advances have been so effective since
2004 that it's now rarely necessary to supplement medicated grit with hand-
worming grouse at the dead of night. "Things have moved on since twenty
years ago," said George Thompson when I spoke to him recently. "Nowadays we
test grouse from different beats of the moor for worm infestations during the
shooting season, and provide prescription medicated grit where and when it's
necessary." And if George were still worming his beloved grouse with a drench
gun, I expect that thermal imaging would have replaced the old-fashioned
spotlight as the best way of locating birds roosting on the ground at night.*

I AM HIGH up on the North York Moors, at the dead of night. The hen grouse in front of me is bobbing nervously up and down in the heather, its jet black eyes glittering in the beam of a powerful spotlight. As I move towards the bird I sweep the net I am carrying down over the russet body, imprisoning the bundle of feathers in fine mesh. But as I hurry to retrieve my prize the ground beneath me suddenly implodes, and I slip slowly but unavoidably into a pit of cold green slime. By the time my feet feel the bog's squelchy floor, I am chest deep in water the texture of raw sewage and the night air is rattling with the sound of suppressed laughter.

I am not participating in some drunken poaching expedition, but helping with – perhaps I should say hindering – an important operation on Spaunton Moor: catching, worming and releasing wild grouse, so that the birds are in peak condition ahead of their breeding season in April and May. My companions are the Spaunton gamekeeper, George Thompson and his wife Jill, who between them hope to dose more than a thousand birds during the months of February and March.

George has been worming Spaunton's grouse seriously for the last three years, and believes the long hours – he is out from seven pm to midnight five days a week during the bleakest months of winter – well worth the effort. "If you are breeding from your best foxhound bitch, you want her in peak condition before she goes to the dog," he reasons. "It doesn't matter how much vermin you kill, or how good your heather management, if worm infestations clean out your breeding stock. The better the season, the more important it is to treat your birds – in 1997 we had a tremendous amount left over, and most were then wiped out by worm infestations the following spring. We made two mistakes – not shooting them hard enough, and failing to worm. I vowed never to lose a good stock of grouse like that again."

The worm against which George wages war is a tiny parasitic nematode known to scientists as *Trichostrongylus tenuis*, but usually referred to by keepers and moor managers as the strongyle worm. The adults live within the gut of the host grouse, where they reproduce eggs that are then expelled in the bird's droppings. When those eggs hatch the microscopic larvae feed on the bacteria present in the faeces, before travelling to the tips of heather by swimming up the film of water that covers the plants in damp conditions. When a grouse nips off the growing bud – a favourite delicacy – the life cycle begins again as the larvae burrow into the wall of the gut. They can overwinter there in a state of arrested development until the arrival of spring.

Heavy infestations cause internal bleeding and reduce the condition and digestive efficiency of the host bird, which can eventually lead to death. Research conducted in the late Eighties by the Game Conservancy Trust (GCT) on the Pennine moors proved that this loss of condition also results in a reduced clutch size, poor hatching success, and lower rates of chick survival. According to Dave Newborn, who was a member of that research team, "Our trials demonstrated the success of direct treatment methods used to control worms – broods of young grouse hatched out by treated birds, were often twice as large at the end of July compared to those raised by untreated grouse. We found the condition of the host bird deteriorates if it is infected by a population of more than 3,500 worms."

George Thompson monitors the worm levels of grouse at Spaunton by conducting his own counts from samples of young and old birds collected at the start and finish of the shooting season. When the population crashed in the spring of 1998, George collected a grouse that contained 28,500 worms, "the bird was so weak that I just walked up to it and picked it up – that was the first time I had done that on the North York Moors. The poor thing was nothing but feathers and bone," he remembers.

There is a technique to catching grouse at night with a spotlight and the operation is most successful when weather conditions are favourable. "The birds sit a lot tighter when it's really dark," George explains. "This evening is perfect, no moon and good cloud cover." As we bump our way slowly across the moor by quad bike, George sweeps the heather with a powerful spotlight and we watch for the sparkle of eyes in the beam, or the brown silhouette of a roosting grouse peering inquisitively towards us. Grouse prefer to sleep where they can hear predators creeping up on them, and most of those we find have chosen patches of burnt ground where the crunch of footsteps on brittle stalks provides better warning than the soft swish of heather.

When he spots a bird George swings the quad bike towards it, and his wife jumps off brandishing a specially adapted net, secured to the end of a long aluminium pole. The noise of the quad bike distracts the grouse's attention from the sound of approaching footsteps, allowing her time to imprison the bird before it realises it is in any danger. The grouse is extricated carefully and carried across to the idling quad, where the beak is prised open to receive the barrel of a drench gun and 2ml of Nilverm Gold – a medicine manufactured to treat sheep against worms but equally effective for grouse. Some keepers catch grouse on foot, often carrying a squelching radio to deaden the noise of their footsteps, but when I ask George why he prefers a quad bike, he offers a straightforward explanation: "You try burning heather up here all day long, then tramping through the stuff for five hours at night."

Before the bird is released, George clamps a bronze tag on its wing, and records the details on a board designed for the use of scuba divers underwater – conditions can be remarkably similar on a wet March night on the moors. He uses a different coloured tag each year, but does not approve of birds being marked with gold or silver ones, which sparrowhawks and other raptors can pick out flashing in the sunlight. When we begin to catch birds with bronze tags we know we have reached ground that has been covered already this spring, for grouse are territorial and do not move far at this time of year. We salute one old hen grouse, whose wings reveal that she has been wormed for each of the last three years – quite a feat of survival considering that last season 64% of all birds tagged the previous spring ended up in the game cart.

We have been at work for well over an hour when a pinprick of light appears on the shoulder of moorland on the opposite side of the valley. "That's the neighbours getting started – *Coronation Street* must have finished," George jokes. Although many moors treat their grouse for worms, not everyone approves, however George believes a succession of mild winters have made the practice essential. "Before dosing was ever heard of, they used to shoot large bags, but in those days we got proper winters, with permafrost up to eight weeks a year. Those conditions killed the worms – larvae can't crawl up a heather stem when it's frozen solid. Now we have to dose to compensate for mild winters."

The lights of Rosedale twinkle to the east of us, but to the north a wall of blackness stretches out towards the hidden North Sea. Occasionally the lamp picks out the yellow eyes of sheep, which merge into a dark head and grey body as we draw closer, and roosting lapwings scramble skywards in a flurry of frenetic white wing beats; we even illuminate a tiny mouse scuttling across a patch of burnt ground. When I grab a bemused cock grouse with one hand, whilst retrieving his mate from the net with the other – nearly all the birds we see are in pairs – I feel I have redeemed my earlier indiscretion in the bog and achieved the grouse wormer's equivalent of a right-and-left. Late at night a rabbit offers an exciting diversion, and by the time it has been added to the tally I am breathing hard, and the chill of Blakey Ridge at some 1,400 feet has been dispelled. I notice George is driving the quad without gloves, and my observation draws a predictable response: "not on a warm night like this. When you see the grouse dusted white with frost, that's when you know it's cold."

When we pass a gleaming pile of grit, put out to help grouse digest the heather they feed on, George invites me to crumble the material between thumb and forefinger. The greasy texture comes from Panacur wormer mixed in with the grit: medicine recommended by the GCT to prevent the reinfection of treated birds. It is nearly midnight when we turn for home, but not before George has radioed his boss, George Winn-Darley, who has been lamping another section of moor. He tells us they have caught and released 28 grouse, beating our tally by five birds. The following day I met the owner to discuss the benefits of our night's work, and learnt that although some traditionalists may not be comfortable with the practice, an increasing number of estates are switching to worming their grouse at night. He concludes; "Even though it is not possible to prove conclusively, we are convinced worming has resulted in many more grouse, and a steady increase in our bags. What we can prove is that dosing definitely reduces worm burdens: recent analysis showed an average of 1,215 worms per untreated bird against only 541 for those we had wormed three months earlier."

The real proof of the pudding is in the eating, and when I next bumped into the moor owner at a shoot he was brandishing a walking stick presented to him by his keeper to commemorate a record-breaking season on Spaunton Moor. The tally of 1,172 brace is inscribed on the stick's handle – the best year since 1886.

Must coursing call it a day?

Longdogs and hares at Prestwold estate, Leicestershire, January 2005

As the doyen of coursing, Sir Mark Prescott, makes clear, there was a world of difference between organised competitive coursing and the getting together of friends and longdogs to catch a hare for the pot. Sadly David Midwood's optimism that the 2005 Waterloo Cup may not be the last has proven unfounded, but the ancient sport continues in Ireland. Despite the loopholes of guns and rabbits, the informal version that so many of us (not to mention our dogs) used to enjoy on a Sunday morning has been driven underground, and condemned so vociferously from all sides that lurchers have almost become a dirty word in the countryside. It sometimes feels that those charged with the defence of our country sports need reminding that not everyone who ran their longdogs in pursuit of hares was a criminal, poacher or trespasser. The vast majority were law-abiding citizens working their dogs on land where they had permission to experience a thrilling variation of Britain's oldest — and once most popular — field sport.

EDWARD AND JULIET Packe-Drury-Lowe are busy handing out mulled wine and hot sausage rolls to the large crowd gathered outside their Leicestershire seat, Prestwold Hall. Most of their guests are on foot, dressed in the countryman's garb of wellie boots and wax waterproofs, however at least a dozen, including Algy and Scrap Smith-Maxwell, Edwin de Lisle, and Rupert Mayo are wearing immaculate ratcatcher, and sitting astride hunters used to showing the way across Leicestershire in pursuit of the Belvoir, Cottesmore or Quorn foxhounds. But there are no hounds in sight this mild January morning, only two dozen lurchers of every shape and size, attached to their owners by leads varying from scruffy bailer twine to smart leather slips. The occasion is Edward Packe-Drury-Lowe's annual meet of longdogs, to which anyone with a decent lurcher and a love of sport is welcome.

"There is a healthy population of hares at Prestwold," Edward explains, "but as with any wildlife they need managing – hares do cause a certain amount of economic damage, and can be a pest. I dislike shooting them, although there is no doubt that properly organised hare drives are highly efficient, and seriously impact on the population. However, by coursing we are being far more selective, killing only the weakest."

The owner of this 2,500-acre estate, on which every conceivable field sport and a whole host of other activities take place throughout the year, also derives great pleasure from seeing others enjoy the benefits of land under his management. "An event like this is inclusive of local people from all backgrounds. If I find illegal coursers here I usually ask for their telephone number and invite them along too, and the consequence is that we have few problems with poachers. And, of course, hares are delicious to eat – every one caught goes into somebody's pot."

Before moving off Edward divides the crowd into mounted followers to be deployed as flankers to guard the busy roads, and those with lurchers and terriers. Then he firmly lays down the rules – two dogs only per hare, all dogs on leads when crossing roads – before handing out maps showing the four large tracts of land to be covered, with a rendezvous point marked at the end of each beat. Helen Connors has brought along Call it a Day for me to ride – a lovely-looking horse that was once third in the Grand National. It seems churlish to decline her kind offer and I abandon the first long foot slog in favour of the pigskin – but strictly in the interests of research, you understand. Two dogs are slipped on the first hare within ten minutes of setting off, and they pull her down a field from Mere Hill after a thrilling chase played out against a backdrop of Loughborough's urban sprawl gleaming palely in the weak winter sunshine. The landscape here is a far cry from the green pastures of high Leicestershire, but the large arable fields dried a lighter shade of brown by the recent gales are teeming with fit brown hares.

When we cross the Stanford Lane to walk the low-lying fields besides the River Soar we find only one hare, but she runs two rangy black lurchers to a standstill in a breathtaking display of athleticism, eventually baffling her pursuers by jinking into a plantation of young trees. Feeling idle aboard the Connors' racehorse I revert to my feet for the long walk eastwards across the hillside that slants down to the King's Brook beneath the imposing red brick mansion that is Stanford Hall. Tucked away out of the wind, the hares come thick and fast here and we witness some spectacular courses – the best of which begins when a small brown lurcher called Elwood disappears alone over the horizon on a seemingly futile quest, only to re-emerge minutes later with two other dogs in attendance, a line of bobbing dots with the brown speck of a hare just a yard in front. Just as she must feel the leader's hot breath on her rump, the hare takes an impossibly sharp dive to one side and her pursuers are thrown into turmoil, the last suddenly first, their quarry now five yards ahead. That hare made good her escape, but another seeking sanctuary in Rigget's Spinney is not so lucky – my terrier emerges from the undergrowth clasping her firmly between clenched jaws, followed by a pair of panting longdogs, their heads tickling the ground after a long and tiring course.

By 2.30pm just about every dog present has been given the chance to prove its mettle, including Amanda Brook's sleek orange bitch, Twiggy, having her first run at a hare. Some, like the slim black lurcher belonging to Quorn fence mender, Andy Nelson, have clearly done enough, but others including the deep-chested brindles owned by Sarah and Paul Turner, look to have fuel in the engine for one more course. However, the spectators – which include *The Field's* Sarah Fitzpatrick, now resolved to own a lurcher of her own – have all but run out of juice, and no one complains when our host suggests we repair to the Packe Arms in Prestwold for a late lunch. This is the cue for Edwin de Lisle to leap off the horse he has been riding all morning and leg his wife up into the saddle – a dubious act of chivalry considering she is immediately required to follow their son Nicholas over a yawning dyke.

It is hard to believe so environmentally sound a pastime will be illegal by the time this article appears in print, but this most selective of all methods of hare control is not something our host plans to abandon next winter – although ironically, the shotgun whose use he so deplores for hare control may have to become part of the equation. "As I interpret the law, provided we carry a gun, chasing hares with two dogs will not be illegal. I'm not sure exactly when the hare must be shot, but how about after it has been caught?" Edward reasons. Let the courts decide on that one, I suggest. Doubtless the courts will also have to adjudicate between hares and rabbits, for chasing the latter with a pack of dogs (let alone two) will continue to be a perfectly legitimate activity, and I wonder if the perpetrators of this illogical and poorly conceived law, or those responsible for upholding it, can identify the difference between the species. A successful prosecution will also hang on the fragile fence of intent. "Maybe we will meet up with the intention of chasing rabbits, and just hope no hares intervene," Edward says with a wry smile.

By comparison, organised coursing where pure-bred greyhounds compete in a knockout competition that rarely involves the death of the hare, has seemingly insurmountable obstacles to overcome if it is to survive. According to Sir Mark Prescott, a former organiser of the sport's blue riband, the Waterloo Cup, the future is decidedly bleak. "At the moment the National Coursing Club is concentrating on this year's Waterloo Cup, after which we have all summer to debate the sport's future," he explained. "Muzzling greyhounds is not an option, as the law prohibits us from even pursuing a hare, and past experiments in that vein have proved unsatisfactory. Nor is there any future in switching quarry to rabbits – that may be OK for whippets, but greyhounds pick one up in a matter of strides. We have even considered coursing an artificial, radio-controlled lure, but in the past it has always been "killed."

The chairman of this year's Waterloo Cup, David Midwood, is equally pessimistic about the sport's future, and tells me: "It would appear at the moment that there are no options open to us, we have taken legal advice and it's pretty bad news. We all love hares and do not like to see them killed, so involving a shotgun in competitive coursing has no appeal whatsoever."

Despite these grim predictions David does not go so far as to concede this year will be the competition's swansong. "We have brought the date forward by a week to before the ban kicks in," he explains, "however we have staged many Waterloo Cups in the past that people have written off as the last one. This year is no different – we are again looking down the barrel of a gun, but we are certainly not running the event as if it is for the final time."

Another unpalatable consequence of the ban is that hundreds of greyhounds will be made redundant on February 18th. For Russell and Kim Gooding, who train forty coursing greyhounds in Lincolnshire, the future is especially grim. "Most of the dogs we have in training will have to be destroyed," Russell told me, "there is no hope for them – greyhounds kept in kennels do not adapt to a household environment, and they are quite likely to attack any pet they come across. On February 18th I will be signing on the dole. I've no other income except from training greyhounds, but I have a family to keep and a mortgage to pay, and once the sport is banned I will have no income at all."

Despite the lack of hope for competitive coursing, it will be much less easy to extinguish the type of coursing enjoyed by Packe-Drury-Lowe and his friends. According to Sir Mark Prescott: "Organised coursing is a static sport – we can't just gallop off over the nearest hill, but a few friends meeting up with their longdogs is a different ball game altogether, and the police are already ineffective in preventing trespassers from coursing illegally. If racing was banned you could never stop two farmers running their horses against each other, but that would not be proper racing. Longdogs will still chase hares when it's illegal to do so, but to me that is meaningless fun – there will be no form book, no stud book, nothing, and coursing has the oldest continuous sporting record in the world." So there you have it: competitive coursing where the hare is rarely killed will almost certainly perish, but the ubiquitous lurcher, a breed whose history is inexorably linked with the lifestyle of the Romany gypsy, will continue to course hares wherever they may be found, just as it has done for centuries.

Highland stag night

A Macnab – or Royal Bag – at Loch Choire in
Sutherland, August 2009

*As the writer of his own sporting memoirs recently reminded us, a true
Macnab must be poached. A stag, salmon and brace of grouse legally procured
in a single day used to be described as a Royal Bag (not to be confused with
a Royal Macnab), but Jonathan Young's instruction to achieve it remains the
best commission I have ever been offered. "Failing one part of the Macnab,
the story holds," wrote* The Field's *former Editor, "but fail all three and it
isn't a Macnab attempt, it's just a bloke having a fruitless time in Scotland.
I wouldn't run that." Thankfully Loch Choire delivered in style, even though
the stag – the estate was first and foremost a deer forest – turned out to be
the most challenging component. My visit got off to a sticky start when I
arrived at the end of an eleven-mile private drive to find that my hosts had
departed following a disagreement, leaving me (and my dogs) with the run of
perhaps the most beautiful and remote lodge in all Scotland. My short stay –
the Macnab was followed by two days' productive and solitary fishing on the*

lovely Mallart — exceeded all expectations. Four years later the lodge burnt to the ground and has not yet been rebuilt. I have not returned to Loch Choire since the fire, but the River Mallart's Coriefeuran pool endures as the place I would choose to visit above all others if my life depended on the successful capture of a summer salmon on the fly.

HAVING ACCEPTED THE Editor's dream commission, the challenges of bagging a modern Macnab — poaching on behalf of *The Field* clearly being out of the question — soon become apparent. Scotland is bursting at the seams with magnificent deer forests, fine grouse moors and prolific salmon rivers but few estates offer a realistic chance of all three species in a single day. So much can conspire against a Macnab — rivers need water, already scarce grouse can fail to materialise, and hill walkers inadvertently ruin hours of careful stalking in an instant. Furthermore, the emblematic quarry species are absolutely wild — they can seldom be manoeuvred, driven or persuaded to take part in the game, and man must be at his razor-sharp best to outwit them.

For this story, Scotland was my oyster but I knew success would hinge on being able to catch a salmon early on in the day. My thoughts turned immediately to the vast and remote Loch Choire in Sutherland, whose beguiling River Mallart I have grown to know and love. Salmon are caught there on a skated fly in the lowest of water, and when the river is full, fish on the bank are almost guaranteed. Furthermore her 32,500 acres, straddling both Helmsdale and Naver watersheds, comprise one of the most consistent stag forests in Scotland and the head stalker, Neil Mackay, has begun rigorous efforts to increase grouse. I was also encouraged by Derek Knowles' astonishing record of thirteen separate Macnabs, all taken at Loch Choire. Mr Knowles agrees with my theory that most Macnabs just happen, they are not planned beforehand. "All mine fell into place through a lucky combination of circumstances," he recalls. "It usually starts with catching a fish before breakfast and taking things from there."

I have been in that pole position a few times, and having caught a fish early one August morning, remember suggesting a Macnab to Loch Choire's late and great stalker, Albert Grant. Albert merely looked up through watery eyes from his seat on the gunroom bench and told me, "I've been here 30 years and not got one yet." In my experience his reaction was fairly typical, not because he ever shirked a challenge, but rather he deplored the thought of a shotgun frightening a single one of his treasured beasts across the march. Albert's gruff manner concealed a kind soul, but I had already resolved to continue fishing when he relented ten minutes later, and my chance was gone. This time there was enthusiasm from the estate's owners, but remembering that gunroom conversation, I next telephoned Neil Mackay who left me in no doubt that he was willing and able to assist.

So here I am, a few weeks later, appraising the River Mallart in Sutherland, the time a little after 7.30am on an overcast August morning. My dilemma is whether to cherry-pick the best pools, or work my way methodically downstream. As she is flowing at a good height, I decide on the latter option and my small Munro Killer is soon at work. Although a couple of inches above summer level, the water is clear enough to demand absolute concealment and I move slowly downstream taking care to keep my silhouette low, whilst Neil's wife, Sue, takes photographs from a discreet distance. I pass fishless through some of the best pools in the upper reaches – Private Water, Jock's, and Lower Alt Fearn amongst them – with only a golden spotted trout for my efforts, and several hours have been squandered by the time I reach Coriefeuran.

Many an angler must have hurried past this short run of broken water in favour of better things, but for me, Coriefeuran is quite simply the best pool in the river. As my fly flicks ever closer to the square yard of smooth flow at the tail I feel sufficiently confident to call out to Sue, "I'll get one here," and when the line pulls taunt and starts to cut its way upstream the overwhelming sensation is one of relief, and not surprise. There can be no standing on ceremony when a Macnab is at stake and the fish – a lovely silver grilse that must have streamed up the Naver in double-quick time – is soon beached. The previous evening we had agreed to postpone my attempt to the following day had I remained fishless by 2pm. I caught my fish with just 90 minutes to spare.

Twenty minutes later I am lying on the ground taking a shot at the target and then we are off to the hill – the party now joined by Ronald McDonald, who has stalked this territory for over 40 years and has spied a small group of stags on the shoulder of Meall Ard. We have spoken little of grouse, for we believe they comprise the most difficult part of the challenge. Although my 12-bore accompanies us on the bumpy ride uphill there is an underlying apprehension that it may remain in its sleeve. But we are about to get lucky, in that seriously lucky way that just occasionally visits sportsmen who pursue the truly wild. At Double Burns a nervous cock grouse explodes from the heather and, as he wings away, a curious black head pops up and back down again as quick as a fisherman's float. Gun pressed into my hand, I am out of the Argocat in an instant, sinking the wind until I am a good hundred yards below where the covey lie hidden. I creep back into the breeze praying that their nerve holds until I am within range, and for once the grouse oblige, lifting well within shot in whir of flashing brown wings. Two birds – one young, one old – tumble onto the heather. To have managed a right-and-left was a relief, for only a brace of grouse will do for a true Macnab.

With the most difficult parts of the challenge behind us there are smiles of jubilation all round – although had any of us been able to canvas the deer's opinion on that assumption, they may have been somewhat surprised. We ditch the Argocat on the summit of Creag nah-iolaire and begin the walk towards Ronald's stags, but the stalk is soon threatened by the appearance of a lone hill walker, as conspicuous as a snowflake on a pile of soot. Neil stifles an expletive, but when we next see the walker she is scrambling back down the scree face. Hoping they have remained undisturbed, we crawl onto a brow overlooking the beasts but they are clearly restless, and the sudden appearance of spooky hinds sees them pouring out of the glen, and with them any chance of a shot.

There is another larger group of stags grazing and resting a mile ahead on the Eagle Face but the ground between them and us looks as bare as a newly mown meadow. The wind may be good, but although the approach looks near impossible there is little alternative but to try. Thus begins one of the longest, wettest and toughest crawls I have ever undertaken, the early stages plagued by swarms of fierce midges that breach thick tweed with impunity and are only vanquished when we crawl out from the lee of a hill into deteriorating weather. Eventually we are within 500-yards of the herd, however these are not October deer preoccupied with the rut, but summer stags protected by the vigilance of wise and nervous hinds.

There are several shootable beasts amongst the 30-odd, some clean, some still in velvet and others sporting ragged strips of dried tissue. Having got this far I am reluctant to take a very long shot and insist we crawl ever closer. Progress is painfully slow, but sure – that is until a meandering line of twitchy hinds pauses to look with cupped ears straight down the hill towards us. There is no option but to sweat it out beneath their gaze, and when one old hind barks like a guard dog I am sure the game is up. But we get lucky for the second time today, and watch them through squinted eyes drifting like mist over the horizon. Moments later we hear the distant chortle of an alarmed cock grouse. "They must have disturbed him," Neil whispers, and we set off like worms once more.

With the hinds gone, we make steady progress until reaching a point when it would be folly to attempt to crawl any closer. The deer are still well over 200 yards distant, and we have been on our bellies for the best part of three hours. With the light fading, it is now or never. Most of the stags are on their feet, feeding into the wind with only their backsides showing. Neil identifies one suitable beast after another but none co-operates until a ten-pointer, his attention caught by some particularly succulent patch of grass, shifts sideways to present a shot. The rifle's roar rolls out through the empty hills, the herd flees, and Neil says simply, "That'll do." We watch the stag walk off slowly through the gloaming to sink into a peat hag from which he never gets up.

The Macnab may have taken nearly twelve hours to achieve, but thanks to the support of three determined individuals I have managed it on the first day of trying – and I feel as if I could walk to John O'Groats and back. Neil feels the same way and together we stride homewards off the hill, happy to be upright on two feet. Mine is only the latest in a long line of Macnabs provided by Loch Choire, but none of the photographs depicting these triumphs back at the lodge were snapped after the light had drained from the hills – a fact not lost on Ronald, who says the day has been enhanced by being taken right to the wire. With rain lashing down on the game larder, we all drink to that – and to the estate's Macnabs of the future.

Foraging in Scotland's Bay of Plenty

Hunter-gathering on the west coast of Scotland, summer 2018

*If successful, the freshwater angler can enjoy eating trout, sea trout or salmon
(although it's a rare treat these days to be allowed a migratory fish for the
pot), the rough shooter might have three or four species to savour after a long
day on the hill, but hunter-gatherers who ply their trade on the foreshore
and beneath the waves can look forward to a feast of unrivalled variety.
Furthermore, whilst river fish and feathered game are likely to have cost
their capturer considerably more to put on the table than their supermarket
equivalent, coastal delicacies are generally and genuinely food for free. And
being absolutely fresh, which is the best — some would say only — way to eat
seafood, the taste is simply unbeatable.*

I REMEMBER THE first time I visited the Bay of Plenty on the west coast of Scotland as if it were yesterday, and the fizz of baitfish rupturing the sea swell beneath a hot blue sky. Shoals of mackerel lurked offshore, and every few minutes they charged into the clearer shallows to attack the smaller fish with such ferocity that the ebbing tide left behind quivering silver heaps on the damp seaweed. I departed a few hours later lugging a rucksack full of mackerel and buckets of whitebait to feast on for months to come. That discovery was made nearly a decade ago but the Bay of Plenty has rewarded the long walk out to her shores every summer since, and offered up memorable sightings of sea eagles, roe deer and seals for the delectation of my family. I am not the only hunter-gatherer to visit the west coast of Scotland for her rich pickings, but I have yet to meet another soul at my favourite and most secret of locations.

Perhaps that is because everyone has their own special place to forage fruits of the sea and shore. The Tyacke family visit a remote cottage on the rugged west coast a little farther south for hunter-gathering holidays, where langoustines are the ultimate prize. Also known as prawns, these vivid orange crustaceans thrive in deep sea lochs with firm sandy bottoms, and are caught in small creels with side entrance funnels. "On a good day our five pots can yield a dozen prawns," says Richard. "It's hard work pulling them up through 25 metres of water and you need a boat to reach the middle of the loch, but they are easier to catch than lobsters and even better eating." The Tyacke's pots are baited with mackerel and they sometimes catch dogfish and squat lobsters. "Dogfish aren't popular because they have to be skinned before eating," Tyacke explains, "but they make delicious fish and chips when fried in batter." Others boil dogfish to loosen their sandpaper-like skin before peeling it off, but according to Tyacke that renders the meat mushy and tasteless.

One April the Tyackes took me up the sea loch to visit a spectacularly remote and beautiful bay where we found a beach bubbling with thousands of squirting razor clams that had been exposed by a low spring tide. These delicious bivalves are seldom as easily harvested as they were that morning, and we dug up several to barbeque in their shells; cooked this way, the sweet and succulent meat tastes like fresh calamari, only better. Razor clams can be caught by pouring salt into the small key-shaped imprints that betray their presence beneath the sand, and then grabbing the long thin shells the instant they pop up from their sanctuaries. Beaches littered with broken razor clam shells are a sure indication that a colony is living close by; however you may not always find them without the help of extreme low tides.

We also found an edible brown crab that had burrowed so deeply into the sand that just a couple of square inches of carapace showed like a submerged red brick. Tyacke uses a glass-bottomed tub to spot brown crabs here in summer and a hooked stick to prise the most stubborn from well-dug-in lairs. The crab invariably seals his own fate by grabbing hold of the stick with a strong front claw and refusing to let go until it's too late. Crabs can also be found in deep rock pools at low tide, although extracting them can prove challenging – it's easier to catch them in lobster pots baited with fish or tinned dog food, which can be thrown off rocky headlands when the tide is out. Beware flimsy mesh traps advertised as suitable for crabs and lobsters; they are fine for prawns, shrimps and tiny crabs but anything decent will tear its way out in no time, as I have found out to my cost. Pulling in an empty trap to find a ragged hole where the catch of the week has made good his escape is disappointing; better to spend ten times more on a proper, escape-proof creel.

The different textures and taste of brown and white crab meat provide more variety than the uniformly delicious lobster, but they are infinitely pickier to prepare. The novice will find clear instructions on how to dress a crab on the internet, and the task is much easier with the help of a specially designed crab fork to prise out meat from the most inaccessible crevices of the body section and spindly legs. By contrast, there is nothing simpler to prepare than a lobster for a quick and delicious feast; having killed the crustacean by pushing a sharp knife through the head simply wrap it in tinfoil, add a knob of butter together with a pinch of salt, and steam for ten minutes on the barbeque.

Iain Paterson works on the MOD ranges on Cape Wrath in the far north-west of Scotland and enjoys running a few lobster pots in his spare time. I joined him last September to learn the tricks of his trade, which include using an echo sounder to identify especially rocky areas of seabed where lobsters thrive. Ian knocked off the engine within minutes of leaving harbour and let down lines of feathers to catch mackerel, coley and pollock for bait, although he lobbed out the largest fish for the benefit of two magnificent sea eagles watching our progress from rocky promontories onshore. We kept most of the mackerel to eat ourselves, for they are delicious barbequed, fried, smoked or made into pâté with a dash of hot horseradish sauce.

With sufficient bait soon landed, we followed the rough coastline south for a mile or more to haul up pots Iain had baited two days earlier. The first held an angry conger eel and some dark green velvet swimming crabs that were discarded, although the latter's meat is considered a delicacy in Spain and they can also be made into a tasty bisque. The next creel contained two large and menacing brown crabs shuffling into the corners of the trap that were destined for supper, but special care was needed to remove them without being grabbed by the strong, black-tipped claws; the trick is to pick the crab up from behind where the pincers cannot reach. "No matter how many creels I've set in my life, I am as excited pulling up my last pot as I was my first," enthused Iain as he heaved another one into the boat, which held a beautiful blue-black crustacean gleaming like Whitby Jet. The lobster was checked for size against a stiff board carried in the fishing box; any with a carapace measuring less than 87mm long must be returned to the water; crab shells must be at least 140mm long and 65mm wide. In Scottish waters unlicensed fishing boats are also restricted to a daily limit of five crabs and a single lobster, and berried females carrying eggs beneath the tail should always be released, along with any crabs that have new, gleaming soft shells.

Lobsters and langoustines are rare treats for the hunter-gatherer, but much can be foraged without the help of a boat. Mussels must represent the most reward for the least effort, for they are easily gathered from colonies exposed at low tide. Mussels farmed on long ropes are ridiculously cheap but never taste quite as good as those plucked straight off the rocks, and the fact that all wild Scottish mussels technically belong to the Crown adds a frisson of excitement to their collection. My favourite beds are a good 40 minutes' walk from the nearest road, which is probably why the silvery black shells of the largest molluscs contain nearly as much meat as a roast snipe. They live beside a clean estuary of constantly running saltwater, which I have always taken to exempt the colony from the dangerous algae blooms of high summer that can put mussels temporarily off the menu.

On the way back from collecting mussels last summer I bumped into an elderly crofter wearing a tartan kilt, knee-length socks and unlaced boots beneath an old tweed cap. Alistair Sutherland was scouring the foreshore for periwinkles – the blacker the better he said – and collecting the tiny molluscs with a tool normally used for picking up litter, having exposed them by using a walking stick to brush aside mounds of seaweed. Winkles have never quite shaken off their association with poverty and the East End of London, but Alistair's bucket full of shiny black jewels inspired me to try some myself, which were delicious when boiled and prized from their shells with the aid of a needle.

Unusually, I once came across a beautiful scallop on the floor of a rock pool the size of an Olympic swimming pool. These delicious fan-shaped molluscs are only found on permanently submerged sea beds, making them easy pickings for the scuba diver who knows where to look, but a lung-busting, ear-splitting free dive for everyone else. Put on a wet suit and seek them out with goggles, snorkel and fins on hot summer afternoons wherever currents mix in clear water, but where the sea bed is within reach of your strongest dive. Carry a spear gun and look out for dabs too – perfectly camouflaged flat fish that lie motionless on sandy bottoms and are delicious pan fried.

I always carry a spinning rod and Toby lure when foraging the shoreline in summer, for schools of suicidal, greedy mackerel can appear out of nowhere as they did on my first ever visit to the Bay of Plenty. Watch the surface for baitfish and look out for seagulls, because even the smallest gathering of gulls often betrays the presence of bait fish that mackerel pursue in a David Attenborough-style feeding frenzy. Given warm, settled conditions these intermittent attacks can last for days on end, which is when a casting net thrown a yard or two offshore can sometimes yield baskets of scrumptious whitebait. As Tyacke is fond of saying, "the whole point of hunter-gathering is that you are up there living like a king on food you couldn't afford in a London restaurant." Not only free, but fresher and tastier too.

Living off the land
Harvesting nature's timeless bounties for the pot during Covid 2020

Hunter-gathering is a perpetual voyage of discovery with new delicacies, harvesting methods and ways to cook and preserve nature's bounties a constantly unfolding adventure, and one that I will never tire of. Had I written this article today a couple of things would have changed. Firstly, having since learnt more about fungi, I would have given space to delicacies such as ceps (porcini), boletes, puffballs and purple-washed blewits, all of which flourish in my corner of North Yorkshire from September onwards. Secondly, my .22 Bruno has since been replaced by a far more effective .17 HMR – any rabbit within 100 yards of that lethal weapon can now be considered safely in the bag

TWO INSPIRATIONAL BOOKS stand out from my childhood: Ian Niall's classic, *The Poacher's Handbook* and Brian Vesey-Fitzgerald's *It's My Delight* for both offer valuable and timeless advice on how to live off the land, albeit not always on the right side of the law. The modern take on foraging or hunter-gathering from the wild (call it what you will, but let's avoid poaching in a magazine of this calibre) is sometimes a bit heavy on edible flowers and common weeds and rather light on feather, fur and fin. My personal preamble though the seasons is chiefly concerned with food from inland Britain (the bounteous seashore having been previously covered) that is the main event, rather than extraneous ingredients that only add flavour to established dishes.

TV presenter Ben Fogle has revealed a few rugged individuals living the hunter-gatherer's dream in wild and glorious isolation, however the modern exponent tends to enjoy a level of comfort that often includes keeping a few hens and growing vegetables – both enterprises can benefit hugely from spoils gathered beyond the garden gate. I will assume a dog in the mix too, for most country people have owned, for at least part of their lives, a working dog of some description. Although nearly all of what nature provides can now be deep frozen for consumption later, that is a poor and shallow substitute for enjoying food in season. The key factors to successfully living off the land are knowing where, when and how to reap the natural harvest month by month.

Far from being the lean month experienced by our forebears, January is now a time of plenty thanks to the huge increase in shooting and game preservation. There was once a time (and perhaps a return to those days no longer seems quite so far-fetched) when rural households were grateful for a brace of Christmas pheasants in the feather, but over the last thirty years their popularity as a present has fallen dramatically. However, the ubiquitous gamebird has never been easier to acquire for the table, and although a roast pheasant with all the trimmings is as delicious as ever, the armed hunter-gatherer may find greater fulfilment through truly wild game such as woodcock, snipe, and teal, which are the rewards of rough and ready shooting available at a fraction of the price of a driven day.

With the game season over, thoughts turn to windy, late winter afternoons shooting woodpigeon as they flight into roost. Not only do woodies provide superlative sport, it is often to be had for the asking, particularly when huge flocks are devastating surrounding fields of oilseed rape. Pigeon have the advantage of being quick and easy to pluck, and there are few tastier dishes on a winter's evening than whole, slow-cooked pigeon. Those that escape the casserole pot can be frozen down to feed call birds in Larsen traps once predator control commences in a few weeks' time, for the best hunter-gatherers are also conservationists at heart.

The roe deer cull should be completed during late winter and early spring before evenings draw out and the burgeoning undergrowth makes detection of these crepuscular feeders almost impossible. Nothing should be wasted from such a beautiful animal, and in addition to the conventional shoulders, haunches, backstraps, fillets and liver there is meat to be cut away from the brisket, rib cage and neck that will provide a feast for your lurcher, terrier or gundog for weeks to come. Do not forget the bones either; these can be briefly roasted with carrots, celery, onions, and garlic before being left to simmer in a pot for hours on end to create a healthy bone broth. When the liquid is finally strained off the mushy remnants provide a feast for hens about to crank up egg production with the onset of longer days and warmer weather.

The dandelions and nettles which emerge in April do not pass my 'main event' test, but wild garlic sails in on a following wind, largely thanks to the delicious jars of creamy mottled green pesto that my wife makes every spring. The recipe pages of glossy magazines are crammed with wild garlicky suggestions every April (before moving on to feature that other great seasonal delicacy, asparagus, in May) and with good reason too, for the flowers and leaves of this British native can be put to a multitude of different uses and are there to gather by the sackful if you know where to look. With squirrel larders bare at the end of a long winter, spring is also a productive time of year to trap tree rats (most agricultural stores up and down the land stock live cage traps that are simple to set and use), but although there are connoisseurs who swear by it, for me squirrel is the wild meat equivalent of stinging nettles and dandelions.

May was once the most exciting month for hunter-gatherers living within reach of a colony of black-headed gulls, which return every year to nest at the same marsh and moorland sites. Their delicious eggs have bright-orange yolks and used to be a spring perk for upland gamekeepers and are still a May-time treat in London clubs and restaurants (not the hunter-gatherer's usual habitat, but we must all leave our comfort zone occasionally). The collection of gulls' eggs is now confined to a handful of sites where 'eggers' licensed and regulated by Natural England harvest the beautiful olive-and-black mottled prizes, currently being offered for sale online at an eye-watering £7.95 each. The poor man's (almost as delicious in my view) equivalent are pheasant and duck eggs, which, as Vesey-Fitzgerald reminds us, can also be used to make a delicious custard.

The Editor recently lamented the demise of shooting young rooks or 'branchers' on or around May 12th, however there is nothing to stop the sportsman taking his own harvest with a .22 rifle or powerful airgun during the fleeting – blink and your chance will be gone for a year – timeframe between young rooks emerging from the nest and taking wing. I am delighted to reveal the traditional rook harvest is very much alive and kicking in High Leicestershire, where the Quorn Hunt holds an annual rook pie dinner from birds shot in their beautiful and diverse hunt coverts. "It's very popular," enthuses rook pie regular and Quorn MFH Joss Hanbury. "The difficulty is getting your first invitation but after that you're on the list for life. I thoroughly enjoy it, although once a year is enough for me. The pie is jolly rich but several guests take some home for lunch the next day."

Being chicken-pale and less dense, rabbit meat offers a conventional alternative to the dark flesh of a young rook and is also the principal ingredient of a most delicious pie. Rabbits can be pursued legally and effectively for 365 days a year; often described as the bread and butter of the rough shot's game bag, there are almost as many ways of catching rabbits as there are recipes for eating them. Ferreting and long netting are two of the most successful methods but are best practiced during winter when the perfect three-quarter grown coney is in shorter supply. My favourite way has always been to lamp rabbits at night with a good lurcher, by which I mean a dog that rarely misses given a fair start and retrieves the quarry alive and to hand. I no longer own such a dog so instead stalk rabbits in early summer with a .22 rifle when young ones are abundant and the grass is sweet. This simple sport demands a surprisingly high level of fieldcraft and is usually welcomed by farmers grateful for help in controlling a costly and prolific pest.

Soon after young rooks have flown the nest the mayfly hatch on clean rivers and streams throughout the UK heralds the start of a fishing bonanza so productive and easy that it has been dubbed Duffer's Fortnight, celebrated in our household by banquets of fresh trout and new potatoes from the garden. Mayfly emerge a bit later up here but their arrival coincides with the time to plant out sweetcorn seedlings, each one sustained by the nutrient-rich head and entrails of a trout buried in the soil beneath it. After June 16th, it's also permissible to take salmon from a handful of rivers where runs are deemed prolific enough to do so, but if you must (and I do) kill the occasional salmon or sea trout, feed your dogs the oily skin to put a shine on their coats and boil up the head for your hens. There is a ford over the Yorkshire Esk where farmers once pitchforked running fish into the back of a horse-drawn cart and led them home for poultry food. Oh my, how times have changed.

If you know a stream inhabited by invasive signal crayfish the chances are that it will be disdained by trout and salmon, for the American immigrant flourishes in the slow, meandering brooks of southern England. I know several Midland streams that are stuffed with the sweet and succulent crustaceans, which can be caught by the basketful throughout summer in simple creel-styled traps baited with rabbit guts. This environmentally sound brand of hunter-gathering is now subject to superfluous regulation, but crayfish offer a free inland delicacy only equalled by lobsters on rocky coastlines. When wandering the riverbank keep an eye open for pigeon squabs that are almost ready to fly the nest, for the milk-fed youngsters are the most delicious, albeit politically incorrect, of all woodland treats. Victorian hunter-gatherers used to secure their delicacy by tethering the young bird to an adjacent branch to prevent it flying off prematurely.

Mid-summer is a good time to dig up wild horseradish roots, which have an eye-watering aroma, and provide a much sharper, earthier bite to homemade sauce than anything available from a supermarket. Horseradish leaves begin to poke through the ground in April and unfurl to closely resemble docks. Years of sparing cherished clumps of horseradish (even our greedy pigs disdain the bitter leaves) when destroying weeds in the orchard provides enough root to keep us in horseradish sauce for a year.

A young August grouse cooked rare with breadcrumbs is an extravagance most foragers can only dream of, but the bilberries on which they love to feed can be gathered by the bucketful on the fringes of heather moorlands. The bucket fills a lot quicker if you use a special comb or scrabbler to facilitate harvesting of a bonanza that is also enjoyed by woodpigeon flighting up from the valleys below. Bilberries are the precursor to a smorgasbord of berries, nuts and fruits that weigh down bramble thickets and fruit trees from August onwards. Blackberries, wild raspberries and plums will be ready ahead of properly autumnal goodies such as sloes, sweet chestnuts, and walnuts: if you know the whereabouts of a walnut tree watch it carefully in autumn, or risk losing the lot to greedy squirrels. On the fungi front, honey-hued chanterelles appear in woodland months before delicious field mushrooms (they smell heavenly, have pink gills and a skin that peels) emerge to provide a perfect post-hunting breakfast in autumn.

For me, no autumn is complete without the taking of a hare, preferably shot cleanly with a .22 rifle on harvest-scented stubbles before they have been put to the plough, although a hare well found, coursed and killed by a game lurcher – it takes a good dog to catch one single-handedly – was once a fitting, but now illegal, way of acquiring a hare. "Only shoot a hare if you are prepared to carry your quarry and take her home to eat," is an instruction often issued at the start of a rough shoot. I am happy to lug the heavy burden all day long for the pleasure of the feast it will provide for up to eight guests. When gutting her, save a cupful of blood from the heart cavity (there will be no shortage) and add it back to the gruel along with a glass of two of the best port you can spare to put the finishing touches to jugged hare, a winter dish that deserves pride of place on the hunter-gatherer's table.

From paddock to plate

Killing a pig at home in North Yorkshire,
November 2020

*I have managed to avoid killing another pig at home since this article was
published but have been surprised to discover how many of my farming
neighbours still do kill and butcher their own pig; it's just they are tight-
lipped about it for fear for being asked to perform a particularly time-
consuming and unpalatable favour. The thriving abattoir I used near York
seemed too large and well organised to be under threat but it also shut down
for good last year. Consequently, I now haul my hapless pigs all the way
through Middlesbrough to the furthest flung slaughterhouse yet; a sprawling
complex with a car park the size of all the previous abattoirs combined. It's*

hard to imagine that one closing anytime soon, but you never know. All the others have. If I were to continue keeping pigs, home-kill would be the only way forward but even that option may come under threat. I would not be the least surprised if such a sensible and humane solution was banned – after all, many other long-standing rural traditions have been outlawed, so why not this one, which is already throttled by unnecessary red tape. Until then, every autumn a new batch of Gloucester Old Spot weaners will enjoy a short but idyllic life rootling for apples in my orchard: but if abattoirs continue closing at the current rate that bucolic sight may become just a distant memory.

WHEN I FIRST started raising Gloucester Old Spots for their delicious pork it was but a short journey from their home in the orchard to an unassuming abattoir in the local village. They had been killing pigs, sheep and cattle there for more than half a century, but after the owner passed away, no one came forward to take it on. The lack of enthusiasm was unsurprising, given increasingly onerous regulations involved with running an abattoir, especially it seems, one that is rural, traditional and small. That year, instead of driving my porkers on a five-minute journey to Nunnington, I took them an hour east towards Scarborough where a small slaughterhouse stood behind a butcher's shop celebrated for pork pies. Next came an even longer haul to the other side of the North York Moors, but within eight months that abattoir had also been forced to close down.

Ironically, regulations that could have benefited animal welfare have instead resulted in increased levels of stress due to much longer journeys. "Abattoirs are fewer and further between every year, and many are not interested in dealing with people who have only a few pigs," laments Belvoir MFH and fellow pork producer, Tom Kingston, from his Leicestershire smallholding. This is bad news for smallholders but even worse for the eleven native British breeds identified by the Rare Breeds Survival Trust, all of which are in danger of imminent extinction. Commercial pig farmers cannot fulfil contracts with traditional, slow maturing-pigs such as Oxford Sandy & Black, Berkshire and Tamworth that have been integral to our rural history and culture for centuries.

I'm hanging in there for now with a fourth excellent abattoir, which has the advantage of being bang en route to my stepdaughters' school, adding a certain piquancy to the monotonous school run. If that is ever forced to close the sight of Gloucester Old Spots rummaging in our orchard will be consigned to history, unless of course, I confront the elephant in the room that is killing one's own pigs at home. When it was time for this year's porkers to meet their maker, it was obvious than one little gilt was, well, just a bit too little. She was granted a reprieve and given more time to furnish out into something fit for the table. It's often said that pigs should not be kept alone, but no one told Cherie, who quickly became the most indulged porcine in Yorkshire. Within six weeks it was time to seal her fate, but I couldn't face taking Cherie on a long and lonely journey to the abattoir. Far better I surmised, to kill her at home in the orchard she had made her own.

Killing your own pig for personal or immediate family consumption is still legal, provided that no part of the carcass is removed from the premises to be processed elsewhere – meaning you must double up as both slaughterman and butcher. The UK government Food Standards Agency emphasises measures that must be taken to avoid unnecessary suffering during the killing process, which can be achieved by either a 'free bullet weapon' (rifle, shotgun, or humane killer) or a captive bolt followed by immediate bleeding. If this is all a bit much and you prefer to employ someone else to do your dirty work that individual must hold a certificate of competence or a suitably registered authorised licence.

As it happens, there is a long history of pig killing at the house I have called home for more than two decades, evocatively documented by the art historian, poet, and literary critic Sir Herbert Read, who lived here until his father died when he was nine years old. In his acclaimed childhood autobiography, *The Innocent Eye*, Read explains how the family pig was fattened on potatoes "boiled in their earthy skins" before being dragged by a rope threaded through a ring in its nose to the Copper House. During this short journey, the hapless animal's squealing "filled the whole farm" until it was silenced by having its throat cut, after which it was stretched out on a trestle table ready for scalding.

No such trauma for Cherie; one moment her snout was guzzling a last treat from the trough, the next it was resting motionless in the mud. We bled her on the spot before suspending the carcass from the bough of a low-slung apple tree in the garden. I say we, for I had enlisted Tom Holt and friends to help with the next, crucial stage of the process. Pigs are not skinned; their dense hair must be removed immediately after death to leave a hide smooth as polished stone that will eventually become delicious pork crackling. The hairs come away more easily after the body has been scalded in hot water, which in Read's day was heated in a copper before the whole family set to work with the feet of metal candlesticks. A more conventional method is to lay the carcass in a bath of just-boiled water and vigorously roll it back and forth with a heavy chain to loosen and remove the hair. Several other techniques can be found online, which suggests that I am not the only one to kill and butcher a pig at home.

Holt said chains and a bathtub were way too complicated; instead of all that, we would be much better off using a steam cleaner. But after the machine's spectacular failure (the steam was not nearly hot enough) we resorted to a relay of electric kettles and blunt knives, which worked to perfection. Read noted that the death of his family pig was followed by "a whole orgy of good things to eat" such as pork pies, trotters and sausages, but fresh liver would be at the top of my list. Along with the entrails, this delicacy is procured once the hair has been removed, a choice cut going straight into the breakfast frying pan, the remainder forming the principal ingredient of a delicious pâté. After removing the head, sawing the carcass into two shining halves, and hanging them up in the old Blacksmith's Shop, it was time to sit down to an *al fresco* breakfast warmed by logs glowing from inside the old copper, long since converted into a wood-burning stove.

The carcass has set cold and firm by the time Holt returns three days later to help transform it into something resembling the display on a butcher's counter. He arrives armed with razor sharp knives, saws and a steel, to which I add aprons and a bucket of hot water, for butchery on a raw December morning can numb fingers to the bone. Shoulders are filleted out for sausage meat, or rolled into roasting joints tied with string, the ribs fashioned into chops and the haunches removed for hams, the greatest prize of home-produced pork. Preserving pork so that it could be eaten at leisure throughout a long winter was well established by Roman times and is practised in various guises throughout the world. Parma, Serrano, and Prosciutto are familiar air-dried continental varieties, but up here in the north is has to be a York ham, dry cured on a bed of salt. I remember huge, gleaming haunches suspended from barn rafters that were the pride and joy of a neighbouring farmer, and the thick, succulent pink cuts he carved for his guests each summer at the Ryedale Show.

Dick Brown had his own, closely guarded, preserving recipe that was reputed to have included molasses, herbs, spices and beer but I have found nothing to beat an equal mix of salt and brown sugar, liberally daubed over the haunch, which is then vacuum sealed in a bag and left for three weeks to cure. Breathtakingly simple but unfailingly delicious, and no finer treat for Christmas or a sporting week in the Scottish Highlands. An advantage of butchering at home is that you are able to create made-to-measure pork: one gigantic ham or perhaps three small ones, the belly cured the same way to provide bacon, or eaten as a dish in its own right – there are choices to be made with every cut of the knife. Keep the trotters too, for there is nothing better when a recipe calls for gelatine. Making sausages at home is a messy business, involving clearing and cleaning intestines so they can be used for skins. Were it not prohibited according to the myopic letter of the law, it would be easier to deliver the offcuts to a good butcher, such as Nessfield and Piercy in the racehorse training centre of Norton, to do the job instead. Unadorned by fancy and extraneous ingredients, their sausages are the best we have ever eaten.

It takes less than two hours to complete the butchery, which is just as well because hounds are meeting nearby, and Holt must exchange bloodied apron and wellies for black coat and top boots. Being a law-abiding citizen, I am unable to send my altruistic helper away with so much as a chop for his efforts, but we have proven the old adage that every part of a pig can be utilised except for the squeal – even the head, which Holt has conveniently ignored. Having been skinned and quartered, it spends a night in the fridge immersed in home-made brine, followed by steady simmering in a stock pot. Six hours later, it's time to discard bones and teeth – and possibly the bullet if that is how your pig was dispatched – settle the residual pork into earthenware dishes, pour over some of the cooking liquid and leave to set.

Over a lunch of cold brawn, chunks of home-made bread and pickled walnuts, it's time to reflect on what has been a challenging but rewarding undertaking. Although I would happily repeat the exercise, I am not convinced all smallholders would be equally enthusiastic – but having friends to help was the key, and transformed a potentially macabre task into one that was filled with banter and fun. Perhaps that's just as well, for if abattoirs continue to fold like packs of falling cards, home killing may soon become the only option for anyone who raises a pig in their back garden, orchard or paddock. For the sake of those unique and increasingly rare county breeds, which have sustained us during good times and bad through the ages, let's hope smallholders everywhere will rise to the challenge if it comes.

Row for Amy

Andrew Osborne's solo crossing of the Atlantic Ocean, early 2023

*I have been friends with Andrew Osborne for over thirty years, so knew that
he was not joking when he announced his intention to row solo across the
Atlantic Ocean, but I was not alone in doubting his safe return from such a
hazardous and potentially lethal endeavour. It's hard to imagine the sheer
grit, determination and willpower required to complete such a voyage, but
complete it he did, and in style. During Andrew's journey I often wondered
how he was getting on, but was taken aback to receive a satellite telephone
call from the middle of the Atlantic Ocean one stormy February evening when
I was out rabbiting – incredibly, I was watching a fox at the precise moment
his call came through. Andrew's target was to raise £100K for the charity
so close to his heart, but once the sale of his boat is complete the sum will be*

north of £200,000, which will provide testing for 2,000 children and save lives that would otherwise have been lost. This is the only chapter without field sports at its core, but is a fitting one on which to end, for so many men and women from the hunting community that Andrew remains an integral part of also raise large sums for charity – but without putting their lives on the line as my former Joint Master did during his gruelling 78-day ordeal in early 2023.

IT WAS STANDING room only at St Gregory's Church in Bedale on a cold February morning in 2017 as hundreds of friends gathered to celebrate the short but joyous life of Andrew and Miranda Osborne's 25- year-old daughter, Amy, who had gone to bed one evening and never woken up. Amy had succumbed to Sudden Arrhythmic Death Syndrome, a rare condition most prevalent in young people where the heart suddenly stops beating without warning. Thankfully the syndrome is easily diagnosed by a straightforward electrocardiogram test, and the most vulnerable can be removed from danger by having a defibrillator inserted inside their chest. In the wake of their tragedy the Osborne family set up the Amy Osborne Memorial Fund to support the charity Cardiac Risk in the Young (CRY). Amy's sisters, Sophie and Jessica, have already raised over £60,000 which has enabled the testing of more than 500 children, helped finance important research and raised public awareness of a condition that claims the lives of twelve children or young adults every week.

No one who heard Andrew's eloquent and moving tribute to his daughter that February day nearly six years ago will be in the least surprised by the news that the former huntsman and current chairman of the Masters of Foxhounds Association has his own unique plans to support the cause. "I was planning on sailing across the Atlantic," he reveals, "but a friend pointed out that if I wanted to raise serious money I should forget about sailing and do it the hard way by rowing it instead." By December Osborne will have left the Canaries on a three-month voyage to Antigua, but he will not be joining a team in the famous Talisker race, or even rowing with a companion to share the workload. Like most huntsmen he harbours an independent streak. "I don't appreciate being told what to do," he explained while making the final preparations, "so I'll be making the crossing solo and unsupported." In choosing the toughest available option Osborne is joining a select band of around 130 rugged individuals, many of whom have failed and a few perished; more people have climbed Everest or ventured into space than have rowed alone across the Atlantic Ocean.

Most huntsmen put on a few pounds following retirement, but the 57-year-old who greets me at his Leicestershire home in early October is as lean and trim as the man who became my Joint Master at the Sinnington back in 1996. Given his punishing exercise regime, the physique is unsurprising. "I've been fortunate to have James Cracknell (the double Olympic gold medallist, who is a patron of CRY) advising me on training," Osborne says, "although I wouldn't like to compare my own fitness to his." Throughout the last year he has been using weights and kettlebells to build up the core strength necessary to row though the rolling Atlantic swell, as well as taking his boat on overnight trips to the North Sea and nearby Rutland Water. "I am also on my rowing machine at home for at least three hours every day – it's almost as tiring as hunting hounds," suggests the former Master of the Bedale, Cottesmore and Sinnington Hunts.

Although Osborne will be well prepared physically, Cracknell has warned him that within 48 hours of his own Atlantic crossing (with Ben Fogle in 2006) it became clear that greatest challenge was going to be mental, not physical. Within a week it had also become clear that an intimate knowledge of the boat together with an ability to solve unforeseen problems was going to prove equally challenging. The physical side may turn out to be the least of Osborne's worries, but unless supplies get washed overboard, there will be sufficient edible fuel to ensure he consumes the requisite 5,000 calories a day. I am shown a stash of high-protein dried food, including packets of tasty reindeer soup, which will be hydrated with a Jetboil clamped onto *In Full Cry*'s bulkhead. It will also be necessary to make 20 litres of drinking water each day with a sophisticated solar-powered desalination unit. As for ablutions – apparently everyone asks that question – it's a question of "bucket and chuck it."

We put such thoughts aside to inspect Osborne's boat, which resembles a gigantic missile with the top half of its casing sheared off and a gleaming white projectile up front for the tiny cabin in which Osborne must sleep and shelter from the worst of the Atlantic weather. The boat's name, *In Full Cry*, stands out in sharp white font against a centimetre thick hull painted in rich hunting scarlet. A veteran of two previous Atlantic crossings, she was built at Burnham-on-Crouch in Essex, by Charlie Pitcher of Rannoch Adventure, who in 2013 set a new world record for the fastest unassisted solo row across the Atlantic.

During her most recent crossing she capsized no less than seven times. Does this perturb Osborne? "No, not at all," he affirms, "the boat is a self-righting capsule with no keel – provided the cabin doors stay shut she cannot sink. But I don't want to collide with anything, that's for sure," he says when I remind him of the Titanic's terrible fate. Nor does he want to have an oar crunched in two by a hammerhead shark or to discover the razor-sharp bill of a blue marlin protruding through a hole in the hull, which were two of many inconveniences experienced by his solo-crossing predecessors.

According to Osborne, keeping the cabin doors shut is one of two crucial safety rules. "I will shelter inside the cabin when battered by thirty foot waves," he explains, "but if she takes in water I'm headed four miles straight down." The second rule is never to leave the cabin without a safety rope attached, because it's almost impossible to regain a fast-drifting boat if you fall overboard. Despite the risks, Osborne will have to rope up and slip into the Atlantic at least once a week to deal with algae and barnacles that can add weeks to the voyage if not scraped away from the hull. But most of the time he will be perched on the rowing platform just 18 inches above the water wearing only the suit he was born in to avoid abrasions caused by clothing smothered with drying salt. He will be sitting on untreated sheep skins, which can be discarded overboard once they have become too salty for further use.

Osborne purchased his boat from Mark Delstanche, who last year became the first person to achieve a solo crossing of the Atlantic from New York to the UK mainland. The superyacht captain and conqueror of Everest has assured Osborne that he is capable of achieving his goal, "but when I explained that I only have one finger on my left hand (the others were blown away in a shooting accident) he predicted that I might end up in Iceland rather than Antigua." The solution is a bespoke prosthetic sling – "a claw for an oar" – built to Osborne's own design which will assist him in pulling 1.5 million oar strokes during the 3,000-mile-long journey. If all goes according to plan, two hours' hard rowing will be followed by two hours' sleep. The passage across one of the loneliest marine tracts in the world – weeks may pass without sight of another vessel – is assisted by prevailing trade currents.

"I must reach Antigua before the hurricane season, otherwise I'll be taken straight back to where I came from," Osborne reveals when I ask what would happen if he simply allowed his boat to drift.

The venture has been facilitated by generous sponsorship from companies including Charles Tyrwhitt, Delancey from Berkeley Square, The White Company, Mills Human Resources from Nottingham and Roccabella Yachts. A chance meeting over lunch in Mustique, during which Osborne sat next to Jamie Ritblat's wife, led to her husband's company, Delancey, financing the boat, on condition that the money raised was used to test children from the state sector. The boat represents the single biggest cost of the enterprise and will ultimately be re-sold to raise further funds for CRY. A charitable Trust has made a substantial donation to the cause and a Just Giving page had raised more than £72,000 by mid-December. "Some pledge money provided I don't attempt the crossing, others on the condition that I finish and a handful if I don't come back," Osborne chuckles.

He is looking forward to experiencing real solitude first-hand – the nearest humans for much of the voyage will be those onboard an international space station – and the time his extraordinary journey will provide for reflection. He will relish being so close to nature and witnessing night skies the like of which he will never experience again. "I'm planning on taking a fishing rod too," he says, "but any catch will have to be eaten as sushi. I'm wary of attracting sharks." As his friends, family and colleagues point out, another major attraction will be three whole months during which Osborne has the best possible reason for not answering his telephone. It will be tough for those left behind, but thanks to a satellite tracker on board the boat, friends and family will be able to follow *In Full Cry*'s progress.

According to his elegant other half, Sallyanne, the suspense is going to be similar to a Cottesmore Tuesday. "Will he fall off, will he come home in one piece?" she wonders, "but this time the wait to find out is going take a bit longer." As for Osborne, the challenge holds no fear beyond the fear of failure due to reasons beyond his control. "I have no concerns about not making it back," he states, addressing the elephant in the room of our conversation. "In fact the risk of not making it is all part of the attraction. If I ever feel like giving up, Amy will be looking down from above and urging me to keep going. This is personal. I intend to succeed."

About the author

ADRIAN DANGAR WROTE his first article for *The Field* forty years ago and scarcely a week has passed since then during which he has not participated in some kind of field sport. He enjoyed fishing, ferreting, and beagling as a schoolboy at Stowe, where he hunted the college beagles. In 1987 he was appointed Joint Master and huntsman of the Spooners & West Dartmoor where he lived at the kennels and single-handedly looked after the hounds, organised the country and ran a large flesh round. In 1990 he moved to the Sinnington in North Yorkshire as sole MFH and huntsman, staying for eight seasons before joining the Quorn mastership in 1998 as only the second amateur huntsman in 300 years. He later founded the bespoke travel company, Wild & Exotic Ltd, initially specialising in riding safaris and fishing holidays around the world, and 23 years on remains in office as the company's Managing Director. Throughout that time Adrian has been able to indulge his passion for all field sports in the UK and beyond, and has written for numerous sporting and national publications but most prolifically for *The Field*. He currently divides his time between home in North Yorkshire, the far north-west of Scotland and the Kenyan coast. *In the Field* is his fifth book.

Other books by Adrian Dangar

THE FOLLOWING BOOKS, also written by Adrian Dangar, are available by visiting www.muscoatespublishing.com

True To The Line (2017) is recollections of the writer's life at the sharp end of hunting, during which he was a Master and huntsman of three very different hunts in three unique regions of England – Dartmoor, North Yorkshire and Leicestershire. *True to the Line* portrays rural lives alongside hunting, hounds and foxes, together with the challenges, frustrations and rewards of organising modern hunting in an illuminating and anecdotal style. This book also covers his time as hunting correspondent, hound judge, conservationist and all-round countryman and is accompanied by Daniel Crane's charming pencil sketches.

"Written with style and intelligence" – *Western Morning News*.

"A pean to hounds and venery that should grace every foxhunter's library" – *The Field*.

"Funny, interesting and poignant" – *The Yorkshire Post*.

Life on the Edge **(2018)** tells the extraordinary story of Tristan Voorspuy, who was described by the actress Joanna Lumley as "the man with no fear." Voorspuy's life as an adventurer, horseman and conservationist was defined by a love of Africa and shared with countless enthralled clients on his company's Offbeat riding safaris, which promised life-changing adventures and innumerable close shaves with dangerous big game. *Life on the Edge* is also the story of compassion, conservation and, ultimately, tragedy. In the last two decades of his life, Voorspuy transformed the overgrazed and drought-blighted Sosian ranch in Northern Kenya into a celebrated game reserve, acclaimed tourist destination and successful cattle ranch. True to form, it was while defending this property that an unarmed Tristan, on horseback, was gunned down and killed, a murder that sent shockwaves around the world.

"Captivating" – *Country Life*.

"A gripping story, funny, inspiring and sad" – Charles Moore, *The Spectator*.

"A true picture of a remarkable, complex man – a paradox of sensitivity and almost brutal toughness" – Lucinda Green MBE.

"Voorspuy's story has been beautifully written" – *The Daily Telegraph*.

The Work of the Sinnington Hounds 1994–1998 **(2020)** is a detailed account of 287 days' hunting spanning the writer's final four seasons as Master and huntsman to the Sinnington Hunt in North Yorkshire. The text describes the performance of the hounds, the run of foxes and the challenges facing a huntsman, together with observations on other packs including the Cottesmore, Blencathra, Devon & Somerset Staghounds, Exmoor, Heythrop, Quorn and Zetland. These diaries represent an accurate and possibly unique record of hunting a live quarry with hounds prior to the 2004 Hunting Act and are published as a strictly limited edition of 500 copies only. There are very few copies remaining.

"An epitaph for a way of life, the more eloquent for being unsubjective" –
Charles Moore, *The Spectator*.

"One is transported to an era that didn't know it was a golden age, but
shines like that now. Beautifully bound and limited to 500 signed and
individually numbered copies, no hunting home should be without one" –
The Field.

The Hampshire Hunt 1749–2022 (2022) describes the fascinating
and illustrious history of the Hampshire Hunt Club from the mid-
eighteenth century, documented with the help of archive material from the
Hampshire Record Office in Winchester, including previously unpublished
correspondence and minute books dating from 1795. Celebrated past
Masters include Thomas Ridge, Henry Deacon, the legendary George
Evans, and John Gray, who reigned for 31 years from 1965. The book is
packed with rare and intriguing anecdotes including extraordinary hunting
runs, the abduction of a notorious vulpicide in the 1930s, and a wedding in
full hunting dress that drew 5,000 well-wishers to Ropley Church in 1929.
The author also reveals the many challenges the Hunt has confronted and
overcome during three centuries of continuous hunting in Hampshire. *The
Hampshire Hunt 1749–2022* is published as a limited edition of 500 copies
only.

"This beautifully produced hardback was a joy to review and will appeal
to a wide audience. In just over 250 pages Adrian Dangar takes the reader on
an easy to navigate, exceptionally well-illustrated journey" – *Bailys Hunting
Directory*

"A detailed history, written with style" – *The Field*.

"A wonderful book" – Sir Mark Prescott, Bt.